Keepin' cookin'! ♥ Ruby Dee

RUBY'S JUKE JOINT
AMERICANA COOKBOOK

by Ruby Dee
of Ruby Dee and the Snakehandlers

Bando
PRESS

Library of Congress Cataloging-in-Publication Data

Philippa, Ruby Dee.

Ruby's Juke Joint Americana Cookbook/by Ruby Dee Philippa;

Photos by Ruby Dee Philippa.

p. cm.

Includes index. ISBN 978-0-9837824-0-7 (paper)

      1. COOKING/Regional & Ethnic.

Cover / Book Design: Benjamin Friesen of Swingset Imagination

Bando Press

P.O. Box 151408

Austin, TX 78715

Manufactured in the United States of America

First printing January 2012

To all those who cook out there—whether you be a professional chef or experimenter at home—you are loving enough and brave enough to feed the world around you.

Acknowledgements

A multitude of thanks to, first and foremost, my husband and principal guinea pig, Jorge Harada; my designer Benjamin Friesen of Swingset Imagination; Scott and Debi Flora, Cathy Bowman, and Carol White at About Books, Inc. for leading me in the right direction; mom, papa and my big bro for putting up with me all these years; all the old fans of Bandoleone, Tango and La Tienda Cadiz—I miss you; and finally, all my friends who have shared a seat at the table, on the back porch, or around the fire with me.

Thank you all for being there from the start and through thick and thin: now let's get down to some good eatin'!

Contents

Drinks

Texas Martini   16

Snakebite   17

Peach Mint Nectar   18

Honey Lemonade   19

Mint Sun Tea   20

Spiced Sangria   21

Sweet Tea   22

Home Style Hot Chocolate   23

Starters

Black Bean Dip   26

Carrot Spread   28

Sliders   29

Steak Fingers   30

Vegetable Fingers   31

Fried Dill Pickles   32

Pickled Cherries   33

Pickled Peaches   33

Pickled Eggs   34

Cheese Nut Loaf   35

Banana Cheese Pies   36

Lamb Pies   37

Bacon Wrapped Dates   38

Soups and Salads

Chicken Stew with Rosemary Dumplings   42

Great Pumpkin Soup, The   43

Groundnut Stew   44

Hearty Vegetable Bean Soup   45

Cheeseburger Soup   46

Black Eyed Pea and Artichoke Salad   47

Beet Salad   48

Creamy Coleslaw   49

Sugared Cucumbers   50

Grilled Corn-Black Bean Salad   51

Spinach Salad with Warm Bacon Vinaigrette   52

Kitchen Sink Salad   53

Sides and Sauces

Baked Beans   56

Potato Apple Bake   57

Sweet Potato Fries   58

Layered Sweet Potatoes   59

Campfire Cornbread   60

Pecan Cornbread   61

Old Country Soda Bread   62

Onion Jam   63

Tomato Jam   64

Hot Cha-Cha Onion Rings   65

Drunken Beans   66

Chipotle BBQ Sauce   67

Raisin Sauce for Ham	68	Kickstart Hash	95
Blueberry Glaze	69	Snakehandlers Migas	96
Pineapple Rum Sauce	70	Breakfast Pie	97
Mint Mojo	71	Minted Fruit Salad	98
Steak Rub	72	**Meats**	
Lemon Vinaigrette	73	Blue Cheese, Pecan, Apple-Stuffed	102
Bacon and Blue Cheese Vinaigrette	74	Bacon-Wrapped Pork Chops	
Horseradish Mayonnaise	75	Wild Game Sweet Chili	103
Vegetables		Venison Stew	104
Sweet and Sour Cabbage	78	Meat Loaf	105
Sautéed Greens	79	Mama's Day Steak	106
Potato Pancakes	80	Papa's Day Steak	107
Winter Vegetables with Cornmeal Grits	81	Lamb Burgers	108
Okra Relish	82	Baby Back Ribs with Apricot BBQ Sauce	109
Stuffed Tomatoes	83	Beer Glazed Ribs	110
Corn Pudding	84	Pineapple Rum BBQ Short Ribs	111
Winter Vegetables with Horseradish	85	Coca Cola Baby Back Ribs	112
Maple Ginger Beets	86	**Poultry**	
Breaking Fast		Apple Roasted Quail	114
Blueberry Scones	90	Smoked Chicken	115
Apple Fritters	91	Fiesta-Stuffed Chicken	116
Cinnamon Apple Raisin Bread	92	Pomegranate Glazed Turkey	117
Currant Griddle Cakes	93	Fried Chicken	118
Cornmeal Waffles	94	Pecan Chicken	119

Contents (cont'd)

Lemon Baked Chicken	120
Island Chicken	121
Peachy Chicken	122
Wild Mushroom Chicken Stroganoff	123
Chicken Pot Pie	124

Fish and Seafood

Oyster Bisque Tart	127
Smoked Salmon Rarebit	128
Cheese Baked Fish	130
Citrus BBQ Trout	131
Sour Orange Tuna	132
Margarita Salmon	133
Tuna Noodle Casserole	134
Crab Cakes	135

Desserts

Blackberry Corn Cupcakes with Peach Frosting	138
Crumble Coffee Cake	139
Sweet Noodle Bake	140
Next County Bread Pudding	141
Chocolate Bourbon Pecan Pie	142
Pumpkin Pie	143
Ginger Snaps	144
Grilled Shortcake with Brandied Whipped Cream and Fruit	145
Burnt Sugar Ice Cream	146
Peanut Butter Chocolate Chip Ice Cream	147
Nanny's Chocolate Pudding	148
Chocolate Cheese Tart	149

Thanksgiving Dinner

Roast Turkey with Maple Herb Butter and Cider Gravy	152
Wild Mushroom Stuffing	153
Glazed Pearl Onions with Almonds and Raisins	154
Green Beans-n-Pecans	155
Simple Mashed Potatoes	156
Mac-n-Cheese	157
Citrus Cranberry Sauce	158

Lucinda Hutson

What can I say about Ruby Dee? You see her on stage and she'll steal your heart. She's beautiful, charismatic, sassy, and full of life. Her *Juke Joint Americana Cookbook* reflects that same passion: like her songs, many of her recipes are original, and she's added her own rendition to traditional culinary favorites, spicin' em up with her inimitable flair.

Ruby's music incorporates elements from Texas honky-tonk, Memphis rockabilly, and good ole rock 'n roll. In her cookbook, she combines ingredients from her life's experiences into a mouth-watering stew. One bite, and you'll want another spoonful!

Some of her dishes are simply down home comfort food: nurturing meals the band misses most on those long, on-the-road gigs. Some recipes are inspired by her years as a cutting edge Seattle restaurateur, peppered with influences from cuisines from around the world. All are influenced by her travels across America, brimming with ideas she's brought back to her own melting pot to share with you!

Ruby's recipes are easy to make, yet full of flavor, freshness, and pizzaz, satisfying for a hungry crowd of late night musicians, a family reunion, or a cozy dinner for two. And while you are stirrin' up her recipes in your own kitchen, turn up her lively CD and you'll soon be singin for your supper!

Ruby Dee rocks!

Lucinda Hutson, February 2011
Author of *The Herb Garden Cookbook* and *Tequila*

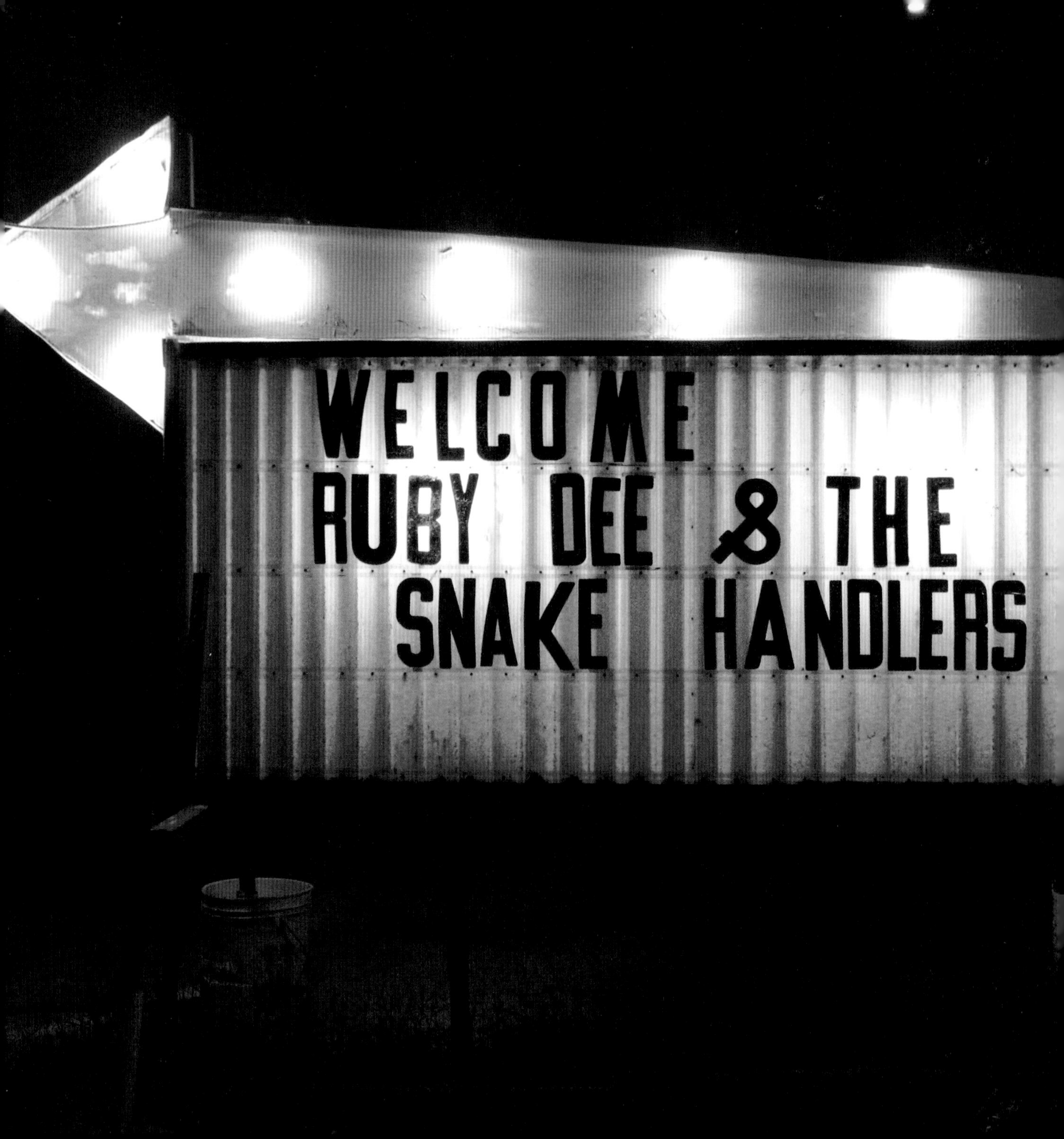
WELCOME
RUBY DEE & THE
SNAKE HANDLERS

Introduction

Welcome to *Ruby's Juke Joint Americana Cookbook*. Go ahead and find yourself a comfy seat, pour yourself a tall glass of lemonade (or something a little stronger), and let's get down to cookin' up some real Americana food for real Americana folks.

Many of these recipes spring from my own imagination and what's in my cupboards. I've spent years making the same down-home dishes for my family and friends—much to their delight—perfecting and tweaking old recipes as I go along. The rest I've culled over time from road trips I've taken around this gorgeous country of ours—whether out for a weekend or two with friends or on the road with my band. From the vast array of roadside diners, back-roads rest stops, and small-town eateries, the very best of what's available locally and seasonally makes up the bulk of my old-style recipe tin at home. I've compiled my favorites from that tin here for you to enjoy with your family and friends on your own back porch, kitchen table, and front gallery alike.

If you like down-home cooking, then you'll enjoy these recipes for a long time to come. The very idea of this cookbook is to provide you with the basics of my personal recipes—something to kick-start your own imagination and taste buds and to encourage you to head down to your local farmers' market and set you on the road to filling your personal recipe tin with your own tried-and-true well-loved dishes. Now, let's quit jawin' and get down to cookin'!

Ruby Dee

Austin, TX 2009

What is Americana food?

Well, I can tell you what it's not. It's not tall, for one thing. And you won't find any squiggly little lines across your plate. What I call Americana cuisine comes from a mishmash of all different types of cultures and kitchens, brought together in one place or another all around this vast country of ours and given one simple way to describe the flavors you'll find there: Americana. From northeast chowders to southwest chiles, northwest smoked salmon to southern BBQ, the dishes and ingredients that go into them are all familiar, all-American, and certainly feel like home.

Some years ago, I started traveling around this beautiful country of ours, taking road trips with friends and touring with my band. I'd buy up local ingredients wherever we went and throw them into the Dutch ovens I made sure to carry with us. The recipes I developed over that time started a love affair back home in my kitchen—between the flavors I could conjure up and my friends and family who were able to help me recall and relive the memories those dishes brought to the table. Over time, I added old family recipes into the mix, reshaping them and making sure everyone approved.

I also write songs about the places I've been and the adventures I've lived. And just like the recipes you'll find in this cookbook, my songs are amalgams of all my experiences, distilled down to familiar sounds. Folks call that type of music Americana—music that consists of many different styles from all over this great big country, all come together under the one general description, if you will, of Americana music. That's how I describe my songs, and that's how I think of my cooking. Try a dish or two and see whether you agree. Even if you don't, that's Americana too!

Happy cookin',

Ruby Dee

Drinks

One of my favorite things to do is invite some friends over for drinks
and supper of some kind—whether it's Texas martinis and BBQ, fruited
bourbon-laced nectar and a variety of savory pies, or hot chocolate and
dessert by the fire, I tend to create a meal with the whole picture in mind.
Are we drinking sweet tea and lemonade on a hot day? I'm firing up the
grill! Are we collecting around the back porch with a bunch of guitars
and beer? I'm putting out a table of pickles, relishes, chips, and the like.
What it all comes down to, though, is: What are we drinking? Well, here's
what we drink around our house. Hope you like these libations!

TEXAS MARTINI

3 oz. limeade (or 1 ½ oz. lime juice with 1 ½ oz. simple syrup)

3–4 ice cubes

1½ oz. tequila

½ oz. dry vermouth

¾ oz. triple sec (or Cointreau or any orange liqueur)

1 stuffed olive of some kind (jalapeño-stuffed olives are yummy)

¼ lime

A dash of the olive juice from the jar

1 Place the ice cubes in a glass.

2 Add your limeade or lime juice and simple syrup.

3 Add tequila, vermouth, triple sec, and a dash of olive juice. Stir to coat ice cubes.

4 Add olive and squeeze in the ¼ lime. Sit on the back porch and enjoy.

The first time we toured through Austin, we played at the Continental Club on South Congress. After loading in and sound checking, we headed across the street to Guero's Taco Bar, where we ate some of the best tacos al pastor any of us had in some time. We washed our tacos down with Guero's tasty Mexican martinis, and once we got home, I made up a version of my own. Now that we live in Austin, we make this any time guests stop by. It's a real Texas thirst quencher!

SNAKEBITE

1 Place the ice cubes in a glass.

2 Add the limeade and bourbon.

3 Add shot of bubbly. If you prefer your drink "up" (that is, without ice), mix the drink slightly with a stirrer and strain into a new glass, without the ice. Otherwise, drink up and enjoy!

3 oz. limeade

3–4 ice cubes

1½ oz. bourbon

Shot of something bubbly (7-Up, Sprite, seltzer water, you name it)

After we moved to Austin, we were given the opportunity to play every Thursday at the Continental Club for happy hour. Those happy hour shows are a lot of fun. They're free, the bands and staff are usually pretty perky, it being early on, and it's nice to step inside, out of the heat, for a refreshing drink and some great music. I created this drink as part of the Snakehandlers' theme for those Thursdays and as a nod to my personal favorites: limeade and bourbon. I'd never had them together before, but once I married them in this drink, I wondered why not. This is a refreshing way to enjoy summer musical fun as a grown up.

PEACH MINT NECTAR

2 c cold water

5 green tea bags (Mom used black tea, but green tea makes the flavor interesting)

2 12-oz. cans peach nectar

½ c fresh mint leaves, slightly crushed

3 T sugar

Ice cubes

Bourbon

1 Bring water just to boil in large saucepan.

2 Remove from heat and add tea bags. Let steep, covered, for at least 5 minutes.

3 Remove and discard tea bags.

4 Stir in nectar, mint, and sugar.

5 Cover and chill for 2 hours or overnight. When ready to serve, place ice in a tall glass. Add peach mint nectar to about ¾ full. Pour in a shot of bourbon and stir. Now sit back on the gallery and watch the kids light sparklers.

★ ★

When I was a child, we used to have these huge July 4th parties every year. We'd invite all the local farm folks over, light off a big box-full of fireworks, and the adults would laze about the gallery, watching all us kids run around with sparklers and lighting anything that whizzed or banged when you lit it. After I grew up and moved away, I missed those summer events. I went back a few years ago, and one of the neighbors handed me a tall frosty glass upon my visit, assuring me that it was the recipe my mom used to make every July 4th. Now I see why everyone came back year after year. My mom would allow tea to steep all day in the sun whereas in this recipe you quickly boil the tea. Otherwise, you're drinking what they enjoyed all those years ago.

HONEY LEMONADE

1½ c white sugar

8 c water

7 slices fresh ginger root

2 c fresh lemon juice

1 lemon, sliced

1 In an 8-quart saucepan combine sugar, water, and ginger root. Heat to boiling, stirring occasionally. Remove from heat.

2 Stir in lemon juice. Cool 15 mins. Remove ginger. Refrigerate lemonade at least 1 hour or until chilled.

3 Serve over ice or pour half a beer into your glass, then fill to the top with lemonade and garnish with lemon slices.

I love a cool, satisfying glass of lemonade on a hot summer day. There's almost nothing more refreshing. And the ingredients in this unusual take on an old-fashioned recipe are actually good for you. They put back into your body what it loses under the sun. A friend likes to pour half a beer into her glass first, then top it off with this drink.

MINT SUN TEA

10 fresh mint sprigs, plus 4 for garnish

6 t loose black tea

½ c sugar

8 c water

Ice cubes

1 Combine the mint, black tea, and sugar in a sun tea jar or large, clean jar, then fill with water. Let tea steep on the back porch or sill, stirring the leaves every now and then, for 2 hours, or all day. When ready to serve, pour tea through a tea strainer into ice-filled glasses. Garnish with remaining sprigs of mint.

My mom used to leave a jar of tea to steep on the back porch, and whenever our kitchen garden was growing full force, she'd break off a handful of mint leaves and throw that in with the water and a varying number of tea bags. This is my personal version of my mom's recipe, brought up to date with real measurements!

SPICED SANGRIA

1 Combine the lemon juice, orange juice, pineapple juice, sugar, and spices in a pitcher. Stir until sugar has dissolved completely. Add the brandy, red wine, and club soda. Allow flavors to marry in fridge for at least 2 hours. Serve in glasses with ice, garnished with fruit.

2 c lemon juice

2 c orange juice

2 c pineapple juice

2 c white sugar

2 c brandy

4 c red wine

2 c club soda

½ t cinnamon

¼ t clove

¼ t cardamom

Pepper to taste

1 small orange, thinly sliced

1 small lemon, thinly sliced

Ice cubes

Christmases, my Mom used to put a concoction of wine, brandy, and juices to simmer on the stove. She would then add spices and serve up cups of hot mulled wine to family and friends as they'd come to visit. One year, on a whim, she made up the same batch of ingredients in the middle of summer and, instead of putting it on the stove, placed the oversized jar into the fridge to chill. Evenings, she'd serve up a nice cool glass of fridge-mulled wine. It's tasty and goes well with just about anything you throw on the grill.

SWEET TEA

5 black tea bags

2 c cold water

1 c sugar

1 Place the two cups water in a pot and add the tea bags. Bring to a boil, then remove from heat and let steep. Pour warm tea into an empty pitcher.

2 Add the sugar and stir until the sugar is dissolved. Fill pitcher to the top with cold water. This will keep in the fridge for a week or more, if it lasts that long.

If you've ever been through the south, you know that when you order tea, they'll ask you in reply, "Sweetened or unsweetened?" If you were expecting an assortment of hot tea, like they serve up north, you have to ask for that in particular. Down home, we just make up a batch of sweet tea and keep it on hand for anyone who cares to ask. Here's the recipe you'll find at our house.

HOMESTYLE
HOT CHOCOLATE

1 Bring water and half and half to scald in a saucepan. Dump in chocolate and salt.

2 Whisk for 3 minutes to melt chocolate and blend well. Pour into coffee thermos to keep hot. Perfect for tailgate parties or bundled up by the fire at home.

½ qt. half and half

1–1½ c water

½ lb. bittersweet chocolate (baking chocolate that comes in "drops" works well)

Pinch salt

★ ★ ★ ★ ★ ★ ★ ★ ★ ★ ★ ★ ★ ★ ★ ★ ★ ★ ★ ★

I opened a wine-and-cheese shop, deli, and bakery years ago that served up this thick, creamy, and downright over-the-top homemade hot chocolate. We would keep a pump pot of it by the register and serve little cups to folks as they came to ring up their purchases. More than one customer swooned once they tasted this concoction. Your family and friends will love it too, I promise!

Starters

What most folks call appetizers I often enjoy as a meal. One of my household staples is always to have on hand one or two of these homemade dips, pies, or other finger foods in the fridge. Then, when company drops by, or I've just had too rough of a day to cook, I pull together a gourmet down-home meal from the different pieces I had sitting around. Somehow, that makes the meal all that much more tasty. And sure! These serve pretty well as actual starters, too, when you need something quick to cobble together for that picnic or potluck. Either way, I hope you have fun making them and eating them up.

BLACK BEAN DIP

Serves 8–10 as an appetizer

A

2 15-oz. cans black beans

1 c chopped onion

3 cl crushed garlic

1 large chopped carrot

1 stalk chopped celery

1 t ground coriander

2 T oil

B

1 orange, peeled and chopped

½ c orange juice

1 T sherry

¼ t black pepper

¼ t chili powder

½ T lemon juice

1 Sauté group A in oil, beginning with the onions and garlic. After they wilt to a soft, translucent stage, add the carrots and celery. Sauté these for another 4–5 minutes. Then add the spices.

2 Add group B to group A. Allow the flavors to come together, cooking over low heat and stirring every few minutes. Once the mixture has cooked for about 10–12 minutes and the flavors have settled down, turn the heat off and let it cool.

3 Open the cans of beans and pour them into the processor, ready with a steel blade. When the cooked mixture has cooled down enough, add it to the beans in the processor. Process for a few minutes until the dip is mostly smooth, flecked with a few hearty chunks of orange and vegetables. Refrigerate until ready to serve, then top with sliced jalapeños, olives, grated cheddar, or sour cream—and break out the chips.

A close friend of mine invited me to accompany her out to another friend's cabin some years ago. We both needed to get away, so we packed up her truck in preparation to head out into the hills. Knowing that neither of us would feel like cooking over the tiny wood stove, I looked around my kitchen to see what I could muster up for grub. I'd made black bean soup the day before and, while rummaging around the fridge to find proper camping victuals, hit upon this idea. I took half the soup and ran it through my processor, and presto! We had a tasty black bean dip to snack on with chips and salsa, both easy to bring along. Now, whenever I make a pot of black bean soup, I set aside a portion for this dip. Here's the recipe. If you feel like enjoying this as soup instead, just omit the processing and serve hot, topped with sour cream or grated cheddar cheese. Otherwise, break out the chips; it's party time!

CARROT SPREAD

1 lb. carrots, chopped

½ T cinnamon

2 cl garlic, crushed

¼ T gr ginger

¼ t cayenne

¼ c olive oil

1 T lemon juice

½–¾ T salt, to taste

Pepper to taste

Serves 8–10 as an appetizer

1 Cook carrots with spices, covered, on low heat until soft, about 15–18 minutes.

2 Puree in processor with oil and lemon juice. Check seasonings and adjust to taste.

3 Let cool and serve with crackers or on a sandwich with chicken and spinach—so good.

My best friend's mother was born in Morocco. As a child, I would wander around their home in wonder, ogling the ornate artwork and furniture that set them apart from all our other friends. They seemed so exotic in comparison. And the dishes her mother brought forth from their kitchen were incredible: sweet, lightly spiced, and full of flavors that warmed your mouth and belly. I remember one dish she would serve to us as we played together those exotic weekends.

Makes 10–12 patties

SLIDERS

1 In a mixing bowl, combine the sirloin, garlic, onion, 1 teaspoon of the salt, and ½ teaspoon of the pepper and mix gently but thoroughly to combine.

2 Using a 2-ounce ice cream scoop, divide the mixture into 12 2-ounce balls of meat. Using your hands, shape them to form small patties about 3 inches wide and ⅜-inch thick. Place on a plate and cover with plastic wrap. Allow to sit, refrigerated, at least 1 hour and up to overnight for flavors to mingle.

3 Prepare optional toppings.

4 When you are ready to cook the burgers, preheat a grill to high and lightly butter the cut sides of the buns with the melted butter. Wrap the buns in aluminum foil and place on the coolest part of the grill to warm while you grill the burgers.

5 Grill the burgers about 2 minutes per side for medium. Transfer to the warmed buns and garnish with optional toppings before placing the top portion of the bun over all. Serve the sliders hot.

1½ lb. ground sirloin

2 t minced garlic

¼ c minced onion

1 t salt

½ t freshly ground black pepper

12 dinner roll-sized small buns, split in half crosswise

2 T melted butter for brushing buns

OPTIONS:

Crispy bacon & horseradish mayo
1 piece bacon per slider cut in half and placed in an "X" on the burger
Healthy dollop of horseradish mayo (recipe on Page 75)

Tomato jam and goat cheese
1 T goat cheese crumbled over burger
Healthy dollop of jam (recipe on Page 64)

Caramelized onion & grilled mushrooms
2 oz. grilled mushrooms
1 T caramelized onion

Smoked cheddar, Swiss, or blue cheese
Cheese to cover burger or
1 T blue cheese crumbled

★ ★

Driving around this great big country of ours, I noticed one thing they have out east that just never caught on out west or in the south: sliders. These are all the best you can think of in a full-sized burger, without the need to fill up on more than you might be interested in eating at the time. And, since they're small, you can mix and match your flavors in one sitting. Can't decide between bacon and cheese or grilled mushrooms and onions? Have them all! Whenever I make these at a BBQ, they disappear more quickly than I think possible. I think word gets around.

STEAK FINGERS

Serves 4–6

2 lbs. beef or venison loin,
cut into 3-inch long thin strips

1 c flour

1½ t baking soda

1 c milk

1½ t salt

1 t garlic powder

½ t Worcestershire sauce

Oil to fry

1 Mix together a batter out of flour, baking soda, milk, salt, garlic powder and Worcestershire sauce. Place meat in batter.

2 Stir to coat. Marinate for at least 3 hours or overnight in refrigerator.

3 Drop pieces into skillet with ¾-inch oil on high for a few minutes. Turn as they fry to cook evenly. When the battered finger is a nice deep golden brown, remove from fryer. Serve hot with BBQ sauce, horseradish mayonnaise, or good ol' A-1.

One of my favorite party foods is something that just doesn't exist in nature. Whoever heard of a steer with fingers? But these tasty little meaty morsels are so good, we've been known to eat up a whole batch in one sitting with a simple salad alongside for dinner. They're a great snack to bring along for raft trips down river or baseball games at the park. Make sure you make a batch of the horseradish mayonnaise to go along with them. Makes my mouth water just thinking about it.

Serves 4–6

VEGETABLE FINGERS

1 Prepare vegetables.

2 Mix together a batter out of all other ingredients. Put vegetables in batter.

3 Stir to coat. Marinate for at least 1 hour in refrigerator.

4 Drop pieces into skillet with ¾-inch oil on high for a few minutes. Turn as they fry to cook evenly. When the battered fingers are a nice deep golden brown, remove from fryer. Serve hot with horseradish mayonnaise, sour cream, or tried-and-true catsup.

Sweet potato, cut into ¼-inch rounds

Squash, cut into ¼-inch slices

String beans

Snap peas

Asparagus, carrots, onion, whatever

1 c flour

1½ t baking soda

1 c milk

1½ t salt

1 t garlic powder

½ t Worcestershire sauce

Oil to fry

★ ★ ★ ★ ★ ★ ★ ★ ★ ★ ★ ★ ★ ★ ★ ★ ★ ★ ★ ★

If a steer doesn't have fingers, nothing in our vegetable garden does either! Either way you look at it, I love making up a nice assortment of whatever's freshest and chock-full of flavor from the garden to make a nice vegetable accompaniment to the meat version above. Feel free to add other vegetables from your local farmer's market—whatever is in season will definitely taste great prepared this way.

FRIED DILL PICKLES

Serves 6–8

1 egg, beaten

1 c milk

1 T flour

1 T Worcestershire sauce

6 drops hot sauce

¾ t salt

¾ t pepper

3½ c flour

1 qt. sliced dill pickles

Oil for deep frying

1 Combine first 5 ingredients, stirring well. Set aside.

2 Combine flour, salt and pepper, stirring well.

3 Dip pickles in milk mixture and dredge in flour mixture. Repeat process.

4 Deep fry in hot oil at 350°, until pickles float to surface and are golden brown.

5 Drain on paper towels. Serve on sandwiches or as a starter along with cold beer and potato chips. Them's good eatin'!

I can't get enough of these. I serve them all on their own or as a layer on hearty sandwiches. When camping, I make sure to make up a batch of these ahead of time to go along with the Dutch Oven-cooked wild game chili, cornbread and layered sweet potatoes. There's nothing like the salty crunch of a fried dill pickle to pair perfectly with that sweet buttery taste of campfire-cooked sweet potatoes. Anyway you slice 'em, enjoy!

Fills 4 jars

1 Combine first 4 ingredients in pot. Boil for 5 minutes.

2 Add peaches or other fruit and cloves and cinnamon. Boil until nearly tender, about 20 minutes.

3 Spoon fruit into sterile jars and add liquid from pot to ½ inch from rim. Add cinnamon stick to each jar. Seal and water bathe for 10 minutes in hot water. Let cool. Serve over goat cheese or simply alongside an array of other cold plates on a picnic.

PICKLED PEACHES OR CHERRIES

4 c sugar

1 c white vinegar

1 c water

Bay leaf

2 T whole cloves

4 lbs. peaches, pitted cherries, blueberries, or any fresh, firm fruit that has been prepared—cut peaches in half, pit cherries, and so on

5 cinnamon sticks

Just about anywhere you go, come summertime, and we are gifted with an abundance of fresh fruits. The only problem is, you just can't eat enough to fulfill those wintertime blues when fresh, sweet fruit isn't around. So, to make up for lost fruit-eating time, I grabbed one of my Nanny's pickling recipes and altered it slightly to match my own taste buds. Then, all I have to do is open a jar of summertime anytime of year. Have fun making these sun-filled jars of sweet, tangy fruit. They make great gifts anytime, anywhere.

PICKLED EGGS

Makes 8 eggs

2 beets, cut in half

2 carrots, cut into slanted rounds

2 red bell peppers, sliced

²/₃ c vinegar

4 T sugar

1 t dill

1 t oregano

8 hardboiled eggs, peeled

1 Boil beets in saucepan. Cook, covered, until tender, approximately 20 minutes. Remove from pan. Keep water, simmering, and add carrots. Cover and simmer about 5 minutes, till almost tender. Add red pepper and cook another 4 minutes. Remove vegetables from pan.

2 Slice beets.

3 Stir vinegar, sugar, and herbs into water. Bring to boil. Return vegetables to broth and simmer 1–2 minutes. Remove from heat.

4 Layer vegetables and hardboiled eggs in quart jar. Pour vinegar mixture into jar to cover. Add more boiling water if necessary to reach half an inch from top of jar. Seal and refrigerate 12–24 hours before serving. Will keep up to 1 week in fridge.

Every Easter, we would go to an enormous picnic, attended by what seemed to me to be the entire county. Chances are it wasn't, but there were always more people there than you thought you knew and more food than any of us could eat in one sitting, every year. One of my fondest memories was of the colorful array of pretty things all set out on the picnic tables and benches before we all dove in. I always kept my eyes open for the tall jars filled with pretty pink pickled eggs, somehow amazed that there were hens who could lay such beautiful things. Years later, I found out it was the pickling that turned the eggs that lovely rosy color. Here's my own recipe, picked up from somewhere out there on the road, some years ago.

Serves 6–8

CHEESE NUT LOAF

1 Preheat oven to 325˚. Butter loaf pan.

2 Sauté onions in small pan until soft. Process all ingredients, except topping, in processor fitted with steel blade until uniformly smooth. Spread into loaf pan evenly.

3 Bake 1 hour. Remove from oven and let cool. The loaf will firm up as it cools, so don't worry if it seems a little loose. It will also shrink slightly. Chill several hours in pan, then turn out onto serving platter by loosening all sides, inverting it onto platter, and whacking it along one or two sides of the pan. The loaf should come out in one piece. And if it doesn't, no worries. You can press it together and cover it with a layer of ricotta cheese. Then, place walnuts, almonds, olives, and anything else you like decoratively in design all around the loaf. Serve with crackers and enjoy.

4 If you are taking the loaf on a car ride anywhere, leave it in the pan until you arrive. Then take it out of the pan and cover with ricotta and decorations. Makes for easier traveling that way.

★ ★

When we hit the road on tour, we always pack an ice chest with homemade sauces, spreads, and sandwich fixings so we don't get homesick too quickly. I always make up one or two special treats to throw into the cooler, this cheese-nut loaf being one of them. This is an easy way to make an impressive, tasty picnic snack that will keep well if kept cool before you're ready to eat it up. We like to serve it with crackers or on sandwiches with roast turkey, almonds, and olives. Sounds weird, I know—but don't knock it till you've tried it!

Butter to grease loaf pan

1 c minced onion

1 T butter

8 oz. cream cheese

1 lb. cottage cheese

1 c ground almonds and walnuts, mixed together

½ t salt

Black pepper to taste

½ t dried dill

2 t prepared mustard

2–3 t fresh lemon juice

2 c grated cheddar

TOPPING:

1 c ricotta

walnuts, almonds, olives

BANANA CHEESE PIES

Makes 8 pies

2 c flour

½ t salt

½ c water

1 medium banana, just going from green to yellow

¼ lb. cheddar cheese, grated

2 T melted butter

1 Preheat oven to 375˚. Combine flour and salt in bowl. Make a well and add water. Knead until smooth. Divide into 8 parts and roll each part into a ball. Set aside.

2 Peel banana and cut into 4 parts down the length of the banana. Cut each piece in half.

3 Roll dough out into circles on floured surface, approximately 5 inches in diameter. Place ½ T of cheese on the circle and top with a banana piece cut in two. Moisten edges of circle with water and fold dough over the filling, into a half-moon. Crimp edges with the tines of a fork. Arrange on baking sheet. Brush tops with melted butter. Bake 12–15 minutes, until the dough is golden brown. Remove from oven and let cool a few minutes before eating.

★ ★

There are times when I just feel like baking. Usually, right after we get home from tour, and I've been away from my oven for what feels like too long, I whip up a batch of these little pies. It gives me that sense of being home and rewards me with something tasty in the bargain. Here's one of my favorite savory-sweet concoctions.

Serves 6–8

LAMB PIES

1 Place 2 c flour in processor fitted with steel blade. Add water and oil and mix on low or in spurts. Add remaining flour and salt. Turn until elastic and clumps of dough form.

2 Remove from processor and turn out onto floured surface. Roll dough out and cut into ⅛-inch thick rounds, 3 inches in diameter.

3 Heat skillet. Add meat and cook about 5–10 minutes. Drain fat. Add onion, peppers, garlic, tomato, and cook 5 minutes more, until onions start to sweat. Mix tomato paste, wine, and sherry in small bowl. Add to pan. Add capers, olives, and almonds. Cook about another 4–5 minutes. Add S&P to taste.

4 Place 1 T filling in center of rolled-out dough circles. Moisten edges with water and fold in half. Crimp edges with tines of a fork. Arrange on baking sheet. Brush tops with melted butter. Bake 12–15 minutes at 375°, until the dough is golden brown. Remove from oven and let cool a few minutes before eating.

10 oz. ground lamb, or chicken if you prefer

½ c chopped onion

½ c chopped green pepper

½ c chopped red pepper

1 T chopped garlic

½ c chopped tomato

¼ c tomato paste

½ c red wine

¼ c sherry

2 T capers

3 T chopped green olives

2 T slivered almonds

4 T melted butter

DOUGH:

3 c flour

½ c vegetable oil

½ c ice water

1 t salt

★ ★

These are the band's favorite tour van snack. When I load up a zip lock bag of these into the cooler, we usually don't make it past state lines before they disappear. If you make them at home for a dinner treat, make sure you also make up a batch of mint sauce to dip them into. The flavor combination is musical all on its own.

BACON WRAPPED DATES

1 package of bacon—I like apple wood-smoked, but any style will do

24 almonds, roasted

24 pitted dates

SAUCE:

1 c balsamic vinegar

2 T butter

1 Preheat oven to 425˚. Simmer balsamic vinegar in saucepan until reduced by half. As the vinegar begins to thicken, add the butter and stir in well. You should have half a cup of thick syrup.

2 To assemble the stuffed dates, cut each piece of bacon in half. Depending on how many pieces of bacon you have, adjust for the number of dates and almonds. You'll need 1 almond and 1 date per half piece of bacon.

3 Push 1 almond piece into a pitted date. Wrap each stuffed date with a half slice of bacon and secure with a toothpick.

4 Broil these for 8–10 minutes until bacon is sizzling and cooked through. Remove from oven and place on plate. Drizzle reduced sauce over the top and eat 'em up. They won't last long, I promise you.

There are times when nothing will do but something salty and sweet at once. I first tasted these flavors on a farm out in Montana while on a road trip with a friend. The cook was from Spain, sure, but the flavors all said Montana to me. Here's the version I make at home, topped with a special balsamic vinegar reduced sauce that makes this an out-of-the-world taste your family will beg for again and again.

Soups & Salads

Stews, soups, bisques, chowders, and chilies—these are all truly basics of Americana cuisine—especially if you're partial to Dutch oven cooking like I am. There's nothing like tossing a bunch of great ingredients into a well-seasoned iron pot, throwing that onto the coals or stovetop, and letting it all cook down into a luscious, savory concoction. Mmm-mmm. And the same goes for salads too. I love picking my way through the local farmers' market, bringing home a bag full of fresh produce, and turning that into one of the delicious salads I have worked out over time. My salads tend to be made up of cooked beets, artichokes, and beans or fresh tomatoes, spinach, and other greens. No matter what goes into a soup or salad, though, you can be assured that it's locally grown and seasonal. Tomatoes in the summer, corn in the fall, squash in the winter, and so on. Feel free to use these recipes as a base for your own ideas and then change them up with whatever you find locally that says, "Cook me!"

CHICKEN STEW WITH ROSEMARY DUMPLINGS

Serves 4

2 T olive oil

3½ lbs. chicken thighs, breasts, you name it, just make sure the bones are off

2 t salt

4 large carrots, sliced 1 inch

2 celery stalks, sliced ¼ inch

1 medium onion, diced

2 t baking powder

½ t dried rosemary

1 c flour + 2 T

1½ c milk

1 large egg

14 oz. broth—chicken or vegetable

¼ t black pepper

2 c water or beer

10 oz. peas

1 In 8 qt. Dutch oven, heat 1 T oil over medium high heat. Add chicken, sprinkle with salt, and brown, about 10 minutes. Remove chicken. In drippings, add remaining oil and cook vegetables until browned and tender, about another 10 minutes.

2 While vegetables are cooking, mix baking powder, rosemary, flour, and ½ t salt in medium-sized bowl. Mix ½ c milk with egg in a small bowl and add to flour mixture. Stir until blended.

3 In small bowl again, mix remaining 2 T flour with 1 c milk until blended.

Add to Dutch oven, stirring constantly to spread around evenly. When flour-milk mixture is evenly incorporated into stew, add chicken back into Dutch oven. Add broth, pepper, 1 t salt, and 2 c water, or beer. Heat to boiling.

4 Reduce heat and add peas. Drop dumpling mixture by rounded tablespoons on top of chicken and vegetables to cover the stew. Cover with lid and simmer 15 minutes.

A friend and I took a road trip some years ago back across Idaho and Montana. Along the way, we camped out every night, and some nights it got downright cold. To alleviate the situation some, I cooked up this hearty chicken stew with dumplings. My friend had a box of Bisquick along on the trip, but I would have none of that and instead mixed up real fresh dumplings right there by the campfire. It was so easy, and I have to say it, so satisfying to say, "I told you I could do it!" You can too —here's how.

Serves 4–5

THE GREAT PUMPKIN SOUP

4 c cooked pumpkin or any
squash will do

1 c broth—beef, chicken, or vegetable

1½ c light beer or ale

1 medium onion, chopped

2 T butter

¾ t salt

2–3 cl garlic, minced

1 T Worcestershire sauce

S&P to taste

Pinch cayenne pepper

1 c cheddar cheese, grated

1 Puree pumpkin with broth in blender or processor. Combine with beer in saucepan. Heat just to boiling, reduce heat, and simmer, partially covered.

2 Sauté onions and garlic with salt in butter. Allow onions to partially caramelize, turning a lovely light brown. Add onions to pumpkin. Add remaining ingredients. Stir well and let simmer, partially covered, for another 20–25 minutes. This soup always tastes better on the second day. So, if you can, make it a day ahead and then simply reheat when you're ready to eat. Serve with a plateful of fresh sliced apples, spinach salad in bacon vinaigrette, and pecan cornbread.

★ ★

I love fall. When the leaves start to change color and it's time to break out those cozy sweaters, I know that some of my favorite dishes are just around the corner. Squashes, pumpkins, mushrooms, and all the flavors of Thanksgiving fill my heart just so. This soup is easy to make and sticks to your ribs when the weather outside calls for that sort of thing.

GROUNDNUT STEW

Serves 4–6

1 T butter

2 cl garlic, chopped

1 medium onion, chopped

1 t ground ginger

1 t salt

1 c chopped peanuts

¼ t each: cinnamon, cloves, cardamom

½ t each: dry mustard, turmeric

1 t cumin

2 c broth—beef, chicken, or vegetable

½ c peanut butter

1 T honey

¼ t cayenne

1½ c buttermilk

TOPPING:

2 green bananas

1 lemon, juiced

3 T butter

¼ t cinnamon

¼ t turmeric

Salt to taste

1 Sauté garlic and onion in butter until soft. Add spices and peanuts and sauté, stirring 8–10 minutes over medium-low heat.

2 Add remaining ingredients except for buttermilk to onions. Mix well and cover. Simmer over low heat 1 hour, stirring occasionally.

3 Peel bananas and slice thinly on diagonal. Soak in lemon juice for 10 minutes. Heat butter in skillet and add bananas and lemon juice. Add spices and stir to coat bananas. Fry, stirring, 5–8 minutes over medium-low heat.

4 When ready to serve the soup, whisk in buttermilk. Top each bowl with a spoonful or two of the bananas. Enjoy your "Americana Soup."

Years ago, I was camping out with a group of international friends in southern California. There were Germans, Swiss, Frenchmen, Canadians, Italians, Mexicans, and little old me in the group. We decided that each of us would take turns cooking dinner, someone new every night. When it was my turn, I realized all I had in my van were some onions and spices, peanut butter, bananas, and milk for my morning coffee. So I made something up. When everyone gathered around to eat, they all started laughing at me, calling my concoction "American Soup" or "American Peanut Butter Soup." Once they tasted what I'd made, though, they all stopped laughing. A couple of my friends even took me aside and asked for the recipe, making sure no one saw them asking. No need to be embarrassed, though. Here's the recipe, and if I do say so myself, it's mighty fine. You decide for yourself, though!

HEARTY VEGETABLE BEAN SOUP

Serves 4–6

1 Boil potatoes in broth with salt until potatoes are tender.

2 In a skillet, sauté onions and garlic in butter until onions turn translucent. Add remaining ingredients except alcohol and sour cream. Continue sautéing, stirring, another 8–10 minutes until all is tender and well-coated with spices.

Add all this to the potatoes and broth and simmer over medium-low heat for another 20–30 minutes.

3 20 minutes before serving, add alcohol and sour cream to the soup. Stir, allow to cook down, and serve. This hearty soup goes well with a thick slice of cornbread. Enjoy!

1 large potato or 3–4 smaller ones, cut into bite-sized pieces

4 c broth—chicken or vegetable

1 medium onion, chopped

2 cl garlic, chopped

3 T butter

1–2 stalks celery, chopped

1–2 carrots, chopped

2 leeks, chopped

2–3 tomatoes, chopped

½ lb. mushrooms, chopped

½–1 c green beans

1 c peas

1 c corn

1 can baked beans

½ t each: thyme, dill, or tarragon, marjoram, basil

¾ t salt

1 beer or 1 c white wine

1 c sour cream

A friend and I traveled around the country many years, playing for tips and free beer, and camping wherever we could set up our tent. We played music every night and cooked all our dinners over the campfire when we were done. This was the best soup I recall cooking up during those days. It's so easy to make and so satisfying when all you've had is too much cigarette smoke and a beer or two (or more) all day since breakfast. Not that I recommend that! I do recommend this soup.

CHEESEBURGER SOUP

Serves 4

1 lb. ground beef

1 medium onion, chopped

1 stalk celery, chopped

2 cl garlic, chopped

2 T flour

2 14 oz. cans broth—beef or vegetable

2 medium potatoes, chopped

6 oz. tomato paste

14 oz. can diced tomatoes

8 oz. cheddar cheese, shredded

¼ c catsup

2 T Dijon mustard

1 c milk

1 In Dutch oven, cook beef, onion, celery, and garlic over medium heat to brown. Drain fat. Sprinkle flour over contents of Dutch oven and stir over medium-low heat for 2 minutes.

2 Add broth and potatoes. Bring to a boil, stirring. Reduce heat and continue cooking until potatoes are tender. Add tomato paste, tomatoes, cheese, catsup, and mustard. Stir and cook until cheese is melted and smooth in the soup. Add milk and stir.

3 Serve with toppings and hamburger buns if you like.

Okay, you can't really get much more Americana than this soup. I like to serve it up at picnics as the "healthy" alternative to whatever's on the grill. It's the perfect soup for cookouts on the beach or a warm home-cooked and fun winter meal. Make sure you serve it up with a bowl of pickles and onions on the side.

BLACK EYED PEA AND ARTICHOKE SALAD

Serves 4

½ lb. baby artichokes or 9-oz. frozen package artichoke hearts

2 15 oz.-cans black eyed peas

½ c chopped sweet Vidalia onion

2 T balsamic vinegar

1½ T olive oil

1 t Worcestershire sauce

½ t caraway seeds

S&P to taste

1 Cut each artichoke in half. If using fresh artichokes, put a saucepan with about an inch of water on to boil. Place the cut artichokes onto the steamer inserted in the pan. Cover and simmer for 15–20 minutes, until the artichokes are soft enough to allow a toothpick to be inserted easily in the heart. Remove them from the water and allow to cool. Trim the tips and outer leaves. Proceed.

2 If using frozen artichokes, allow the package to thaw, then cut the hearts in half.

3 Combine hearts with black eyed peas, onion, vinegar, oil, Worcestershire sauce, and caraway seeds. Season with salt and pepper.

This is one of my favorite spring salads, when artichokes first come into season. You can make it anytime of year, though, using frozen artichoke hearts. Another nice thing about this salad is that it can be served cold alongside peachy chicken or heated and served warm to accompany bacon-wrapped pork chops. No matter how you serve it, though, you'll enjoy the tangy flavors from down home.

BEET SALAD

Serves 4

1 lb. beets, sliced and boiled

1 cucumber, sliced

½ c yogurt

¼ c olive oil

⅛ bunch scallions

1 cl garlic, crushed

¼ c red wine vinegar

S&P to taste

1 Mix all ingredients in bowl together. Allow to settle so the flavors mix a little. Enjoy!

I first made this salad when I was camping with a friend some years ago and we passed a vegetable stand on the highway. We stopped, bought some beets, and proceeded to our campsite. I threw the beets into the Dutch oven to cook through, and after we'd cooled off in the river and the beets had cooled off from cooking, I tossed all these ingredients together to make this delicious sweet-tart salad. We dined on beets, cornbread, and smoked chicken that night. And it was good.

Serves 6

CREAMY COLESLAW

1 Stir together mayonnaise, vinegar, sugar, caraway seeds, and salt in a large mixing bowl. Add cabbage and carrots to the dressing. Toss gently to coat. Cover and chill prior to serving.

½ c mayonnaise

1 T white vinegar

1–2 t sugar

½ t caraway seeds

¼ t salt

3 c finely shredded green cabbage

1 c finely shredded red cabbage

1 c finely shredded carrot, if you like

★ ★

There are two types of people in this world—those who prefer a more vinegary crisp-textured coleslaw and those who prefer a creamier, sweeter version. I belong to the latter group. Although I certainly enjoy vinegary pickled dishes, my ideal slaw just coats your tongue and cools any heat you might have going on from spices in the BBQ sauce. I hope you like this old-fashioned recipe I found in Grandma's recipe file. I sure do!

49

SUGARED CUCUMBERS

¼ c white vinegar

2 T sugar

¼ t caraway

¼ t celery seeds

S&P to taste

1 large cucumber, thinly sliced

Serves 2

1 Combine vinegar, sugar, caraway, celery seeds and S&P as you like in a bowl. Toss in the cucumbers and stir to coat. Cover and chill for 2 hours or overnight. Serve with lamb burgers or any BBQ dish.

My mom used to make pickles every year. My favorite was when she would have too many cucumbers to jar up, so she would toss them in a bowl with vinegar and sugar, let them rest, and then we would eat them alongside whatever we had for dinner the rest of that week. Here's my slightly changed version of that simple recipe.

Serves 4

GRILLED CORN-BLACK BEAN SALAD

1 chipotle chili, minced

1 ear fresh corn

1 can black beans

½ t dried oregano

2–3 t fresh cilantro, chopped

¾ t sugar

¼ c olive oil

2 T cider vinegar

S&P to taste

1 Blanch the corn for 1 minute, then grill for approximately 3 minutes, turning on the grill to scorch the kernels evenly. Combine all the ingredients in a large mixing bowl, cutting the corn in along with everything else. Toss to evenly coat and cover and chill for at least an hour before serving.

The summertime salsa-like take on this salad makes it a perfect match to accompany fiesta-stuffed chicken or pineapple-rum BBQ ribs. The key to this recipe is blanching the corn first before grilling it, which brings out its full sweetness. I make this at home throughout the summer, with variations on what I put in it. Feel free to add diced peppers, grilled shrimp, tomatoes, okra—you name it! The star of the show is the corn, and you just can't change that.

SPINACH SALAD WITH WARM BACON VINAIGRETTE

Serves 4

3 strips bacon, cut into ¼-inch pieces

2 T olive oil

1 shallot, minced

2 T sherry vinegar

1 T whole grain mustard

½ t dried thyme

2–4 small plums, quartered

5 oz. baby spinach

S&P to taste

¼ c sliced almonds

2 oz. crumbled blue cheese

1 In a large skillet, cook the bacon in the olive oil until browned and nicely crisp. Do not let Jorge eat the bacon. Remove from the heat and stir in shallot, vinegar, mustard, and thyme. Scrape dressing into large bowl.

2 Add plums and spinach, season with salt and pepper. Toss. Add the nuts and blue cheese and toss again. Serve it up but don't tell them there's vegetables or fruit in it!

Is it really still a salad if you put bacon in it? My guitar player/husband Jorge says, "You bet!" This is how we get 'em to eat salad down on the farm. It's such a tasty way to enjoy fresh spinach and to sneak vegetables and even fruit on the unwary when need be.

Serves 4

KITCHEN SINK SALAD

1 Whisk all salad dressing ingredients together. Set aside.

2 Steam peas and corn. Meanwhile, cook the sausages in a small skillet until sizzling and cooked through. Cut into ½-inch pieces.

3 In large bowl, break off bite-sized pieces of romaine. Add all other ingredients. Drizzle dressing over the top to the desired amount and toss. The steamed peas and corn and cooked sausage will cause the chèvre goat cheese to melt a bit. That's good. Add cucumbers, avocado, steamed green beans, wasabi peas, whatever sounds good to you.

1 bunch romaine lettuce

1–2 tomatoes, diced

2 roasted potatoes, quartered

2 carrots, shredded or diced

12 olives, sliced—any type will do

¼ c almonds, sliced or not

1 c peas

1 c corn

¼ c raisins, currants, or cranberries

½ pear or apple, sliced

½ c chèvre goat cheese, crumbled

2 link sausages—we like chicken apple sausage for this salad

DRESSING:

½ c olive oil

¼ c sherry vinegar

1 cl garlic, minced

1 t sugar

1 t mustard, Dijon or whole grain

1 T shallot, minced

S&P to taste

This is a simple recipe that's really just another way to clean out the last of whatever you have in the garden to make room for something new. On hot summer nights when I'm really not in any mood to cook, I toss together a quick salad out of various ingredients and call it dinner. You can create variations of your own with whatever you have on hand. Just don't forget the bacon or sausage, or Jorge won't come to the table!

Breakfast Pie (1-11" tart)

Tart Dough
1 3/4 c Flour   1 t chile powder
3/4 t salt   1/2 t cumin
9 T butter
4-5 T ice water

1/4 c butter   1 sausage, chopped
2 t garlic, minced   6 eggs, beaten
1 onion, chopped   1 c cheddar, grated
1 can gr chiles, ch.   S + P
4 tomatoes, ch.   1/4 t oregano
                       1/4 t cumin
                       sour cream

Sides & Sauces

What would Americana cuisine be without the wonderful myriad of side dishes we all know and love from holidays or simple family meals? I'm talking about baked beans, cornbread, stuffing, and a whole lineup of tasty rubs, sauces, jams, and more to add extra zip to an everyday meal. Time to mix and match flavors, according to what you like best. Have fun with these recipes!

BAKED BEANS

Serves 4–6

1 lb. navy beans

½ t baking soda

½ lb. bacon, cut into 1-inch pieces

1 medium onion, chopped roughly

2 bay leaves

⅓ c brown sugar

⅓ c molasses

¼ c apple cider vinegar

1 t dry mustard

1 t salt

½ t black pepper

3 c broth—beef, chicken, or vegetable

1 Soak beans overnight. In morning, preheat oven to 325˚.

2 Fill 2½ qt. Dutch oven halfway full with water. Add soda and boil. Add beans and allow to return to boil for 10 minutes. Drain beans and set aside.

3 Place half the bacon into Dutch oven with onion. Add beans and bay leaves. Top with remaining pork. In a medium bowl, mix sugar, molasses, vinegar, mustard, and S&P with broth. Pour over beans. Cover and bake 6 hours, adding additional water as needed to prevent the tops of beans from drying out.

On yet another camping trip a few years ago, I hiked out over tricky deer trails with a Dutch oven and ingredients to make this dish. It rained the entire weekend, so we were happy indeed to have a hot "home-cooked" meal to warm our bellies. I wrote the recipe down for cooking at home. I hope you like the sweet-tangy flavors—they go well with summer BBQ and winter meatloaf alike.

Serves 6

POTATO APPLE BAKE

1 Heat oven to 350˚. In medium skillet over medium heat, sauté onions in oil for about 7 minutes, until they sweat. Add sugar and cook for 2 more minutes. Add thyme and cook another minute. Transfer to large bowl and let cool.

2 Mix the eggs, fontina, paprika, S&P, and apple in a large bowl and set aside.

3 Grate potatoes into a colander and squeeze out excess moisture by pressing down on the grated potato. Add the cooled onion mixture, grated apples, and grated potatoes into the egg mixture and stir to combine.

4 Lightly coat an 8x8 or similar sized baking dish with butter. Set the dish in the oven to warm for 10 minutes. Remove from the oven, spread the potato mixture into the hot dish, top with parmesan cheese, and bake for 50 minutes, until the top is crispy golden brown. Allow to cool slightly before serving.

1 T olive oil

1 medium onion, chopped

1 T brown sugar

½ t dried thyme

3 eggs

1 c fontina cheese, grated

1 t paprika

1 t salt

½ t black pepper

1 Granny Smith apple, cored and grated

2 Russet potatoes, immersed in cold water

3 T parmesan cheese

As a child, on Fridays I would head over to Grandma's house. She inevitably had a feast prepared, usually setting out much more food than either of us could consume. For the next few days, I would swing by the kitchen and cut myself a piece of this gorgeous savory baked dish. Hot or cold, it satisfies. Nowadays, I like to serve it alongside apple-roasted quail or bacon-wrapped stuffed pork chops. Then the next morning, we warm up a couple of slices to start our day out right.

SWEET POTATO FRIES

Serves 4–6

1–1½ lbs. sweet potatoes

¼ c olive oil

½ t kosher salt

½ t paprika

¼ t cinnamon

1 Preheat oven to 425 degrees. Line a baking sheet with aluminum foil.

2 Peel the sweet potatoes. Cut into strips that are about half an inch wide on each side.

3 Place the sweet potatoes into a large mixing bowl. Add oil, salt, paprika, and cinnamon. Stir to thoroughly coat the fries. Spread the fries out onto the baking sheet in a single layer.

4 Cook for 30 minutes, turning once, until slightly browned. Transfer immediately to a paper towel-lined plate and serve warm.

I attended a friend's wedding with a few other friends in Flagstaff a few years ago. We camped out just outside of town and came down into town for the wedding a day early. Walking around town, we came across this very kitchy but also very cool BBQ joint that served up the very best sweet potato fries I'd ever had. This is my approximation of that dish.

Serves 4–6

LAYERED SWEET POTATOES

2 onions, sliced

4 T brown sugar

S&P to taste

4 lbs. sweet potatoes, sliced

⅓ c maple syrup

⅓ c butter

4 t dried thyme

1 Arrange ½ onion slices in bottom of 12-inch Dutch oven. Sprinkle with sugar and S&P. Add ½ sweet potato slices. Repeat.

2 Combine maple syrup, butter, and thyme. Pour over the potatoes. Bake covered at 400˚ for 1 hour or until potatoes are tender.

★ ★

Here's one of my favorite fall dishes. I first made this on one of our nights off out on the road. We pulled into a campground and started a fire. I just threw all the ingredients into the pot and sat back while the Dutch oven did all the work for me. In one hour we had one of the finest simple dinners I could remember eating in a while. Enjoy this with my Mama's Day Steak, and you'll be set right.

CAMPFIRE CORNBREAD

2½ c flour

1½ c cornmeal

½ c sugar

4 t baking powder

1 t salt

2 c milk

½ c butter

2 eggs

1 can creamed corn or 1 c fresh

1 small can green chilies, diced

Serves 4–6

1 If cooking at home, preheat oven to 400˚.

2 Combine dry ingredients. Add wet ingredients into the mix. Stir and pour into 12-inch Dutch oven.

3 Bake 25–30 minutes, until lightly browned and crusty on top.

4 If cooking over coals, place 9–10 beneath the oven and 6–8 on top. Bake the same length of time, periodically checking both the doneness of the bread and the heat from the coals.

Don't be fooled by the name. You can easily make this at home or out on the trail. The flavors are sweet yet savory at once and embarrassingly addictive. I often make a batch of cornbread just to have sitting around in case anyone feels faint from hunger!

Serves 4–6

PECAN CORNBREAD

4 T butter

1¼ c buttermilk

1 egg, beaten

½ t vanilla extract

1 T bourbon—you can use tequila
if you prefer

¾ c cornmeal

1¼ c flour

1 t baking soda

1 t baking powder

2 T sugar

¾ t salt

½ c coarsely chopped pecans

1 Preheat oven to 350˚. Melt butter in small skillet. Pour butter into large mixing bowl and let cool slightly. Whisk in buttermilk, egg, vanilla, and bourbon.

2 In another mixing bowl, combine dry ingredients and pecans. Add dry ingredients to butter mixture and stir to blend. Pour into greased 10-inch Dutch oven. Cover and place in oven to bake for 30 minutes or until golden brown and a toothpick inserted in the middle of the bread comes out clean. Allow to cool slightly before serving.

Here's another version of cornbread I make to go along with sour orange tuna, or to sop up the juices from a whole bevy of salads. I sometimes make a batch of this for our first day out on tour. It helps ease us into those long drives between gigs.

OLD COUNTRY SODA BREAD

Serves 4–6

2 c unbleached flour

2 c whole wheat flour

1 t salt

1 t baking soda

1 T brown sugar

¼ c butter, cut into pea-sized pieces

½ c currants

1⅔ c buttermilk

1 egg

1 Mix dry ingredients together. Add butter and firmly mix until you have a coarse meal. Add currants and mix. Add buttermilk and egg. Knead until smooth.

2 Shape into ball and place in a greased 10-inch Dutch oven. Brush the top with butter and, using a knife, cut an X into the top, about half an inch deep. Bake for 5 minutes at 450˚. Reduce heat to 350˚ and bake 40–45 minutes longer or when the top gives a nice hollow sound when you thump it with your finger. Remove from oven and allow to cool slightly before serving.

On one tour around the country, my friend Marc and I brought provisions to make hearty sandwiches from Irish soda bread and cold cuts. Once we got home from that tour, I started making my own version of that bread at home. Feel free to omit the currants and add caraway or some other spices to give the bread a slightly more savory flavor. This is my favorite version and goes so well with leftover turkey at Thanksgiving.

Serves 4–6

ONION JAM

2 T canola oil

2 large yellow onions, thinly sliced

2 large red onions, thinly sliced

2 c green onions, chopped

½ c balsamic vinegar

¼ c packed brown sugar

1 Heat the oil in a large skillet over medium heat. Add the yellow and red onions. Cook, stirring, for 5 minutes. Add the green onions and stir. Cook mixture for another 25–30 minutes, until browned and slightly caramelized.

2 Add balsamic vinegar and sugar and reduce heat. Simmer for 10–12 minutes until most of the liquid evaporates. Remove from heat. Chill before serving.

I always keep at least a few pickled or cooked down condiments to spice up any spur of the moment meal. This onion jam is one of my favorites. I've folded it into meatloaf or just thrown a touch on top of a batch of sliders or tasty lamb burgers. No matter what you do with it, enjoy.

TOMATO JAM

Serves 6–8

3 lbs. ripe tomatoes, chopped

¼ c sugar

1 Place the tomatoes and sugar in a large, heavy pot and cook uncovered over low heat for 1½ to 2 hours. You can raise the heat toward the end of the cooking time to speed things up. Stir often so the tomatoes don't stick to the bottom of the pot and burn. Cool to room temperature.

This here's another one of those jams I keep in the fridge to have on hand in a pinch. It's mighty tasty on grilled brats with a pickle on the side. Folks have been known to spread cream cheese on a cracker and top it with this jam too. It's that versatile and oh-so-easy to make. Just don't tell anyone how easy it is, and they'll be so impressed.

HOT CHA-CHA ONION RINGS

Serves 6–8

1 Slice onions into ½-inch slices and layer in baking dish.

2 Beat together milk and egg and pour over onions.

3 Mix flour, chili powder, cumin, paprika, and sugar in large bowl.

4 Lift onions out of milk mixture, allowing excess moisture to drain off. Toss onions gently in the flour mixture until well coated.

5 Fry onions in deep fryer or ¾-inch hot oil until golden brown. Remove and drain on towels. Season with S&RP.

3 medium sweet onions, sliced

1 c milk

1 egg

1 c all-purpose flour

3 T chili powder

2 T cumin

1 T paprika

3 t sugar

Oil

Salt and red pepper

When my Grandma Edie passed away, I left the family gathering by train and wrote a cha-cha for Edie en route home. Folks on the train glanced at me askew, as I was crying and singing to myself, getting the song right. Once I got home, I made up a batch of these onion rings since I'd been craving something fried and spicy. I call these Hot Cha-Cha onion rings in honor of Grandma Edie and the song she inspired.

DRUNKEN BEANS

Serves 6–8

3 c pinto beans, rinsed

3 c kidney beans, rinsed

1 lg. onion, chopped

2 cl garlic, minced

1 lg. tomato, chopped

2 sm. jalapeño peppers, chopped

1½ t cumin

2 bay leaves

1 T brown sugar

1 c light beer

Water or broth—beef, chicken, or vegetable

S&P

1 Soak beans overnight. Drain and rinse.

2 Heat oil in 12-inch Dutch oven over medium heat. Add onion, garlic, and tomato. Cook 10 minutes to soften the vegetables.

3 Add jalapeño, cumin, and bay leaves; stir to combine.

4 Add beans, beer, water or broth to cover beans. Bring to a boil, then reduce, cover and simmer for 2 hours.

5 S&P to taste. Serve with rice and whatever's on the grill!

When we're on tour, I long for my grill back home. No matter what time of year it is, as soon as we finish the tour, I fire up the grill and make a batch of these drunken beans to go along with whatever I char out there. Whether that's coca-cola ribs or stout-glazed smoked pork chops, it all tastes better with these beans on the side.

CHIPOTLE BBQ SAUCE

¼ c chipotle peppers in adobo sauce

1 c orange juice

Juice from half a lime

1 T olive oil

1 small onion, chopped

3 cl garlic, minced

1 c catsup

3 T white vinegar

3 T molasses

3 T brown sugar

1 T Worcestershire sauce

1 Place peppers with their sauce in blender. Cover and blend until smooth.

2 Cook onion and garlic in medium saucepan with oil over medium-high heat until tender, about 2–3 minutes. Stir in chipotle mixture, orange and lime juice, catsup, vinegar, molasses, brown sugar, and Worcestershire sauce. Bring to boil, then reduce heat. Simmer, uncovered, stirring often, for about 10 minutes, until sauce has thickened and tastes right.

★ ★

Everybody has their own personal take on BBQ sauce. Here's mine. I love the tangy zip of citrus paired with a little heat from the chilies and the sweet cooling action of brown sugar.

RAISIN SAUCE FOR HAM

Covers one 3–5 lbs. ham

½ c brown sugar

2 t cornstarch

1 t dry mustard

1 T white vinegar

1 c raisins

¼ t lemon zest and 1 T lemon juice

1½ c water

1 Stir together first 3 ingredients in saucepan. Add vinegar. Over medium heat, add remaining ingredients and cook, stirring frequently, for about 10 minutes until the sauce looks shiny and like a glaze.

2 Glaze the ham, bake for 1 hour, brushing with glaze every 10 minutes.

★ ★

Whenever we go on the road, my biggest weakness is glazed ham for breakfast. Every diner we pour ourselves into, the first thing I do is look around for the telltale signs of a good glazed ham steak on the plates around us. Of course, searching the menu doesn't hurt either. This is my home version of that diner breakfast staple. Just pick up a smoked ham, glaze it with this sauce, pop it in the oven to bake for 1 hour at 350, and you'll be golden.

Makes 4 servings

BLUEBERRY GLAZE

½ c blueberry preserves

¼ c port or other sweet wine

3 T balsamic vinegar

1 t butter

1 chipotle pepper, minced

1 Combine jam, wine, vinegar, and pepper in a small saucepan over medium heat. Bring just to boiling, stirring frequently. Reduce heat to medium-low. Simmer, uncovered, for about 15 minutes, until sauce has thickened and reduced to ½ c. Remove from heat, add butter, and stir to blend.

2 Drizzle over any wild bird or even on grilled sausages.

A friend heads out to the hills every year and brings back a bagful of ducks, pheasant, quail—you name it. This glaze is something I came up with to liven up our standard fare and use up some of the blueberry preserves I'd put up the summer before.

PINEAPPLE RUM SAUCE

Makes 4 servings

1 c dark rum

2 T Worcestershire sauce

¼ c pineapple juice

2 T cider vinegar

½ c tomato sauce

1 T dry mustard

¼ c molasses

2 T olive oil

3 cl garlic, minced

3 T lime juice

S&P to taste

1 T butter

1 Place the pork chops or chicken in a non-reactive baking dish. Mix the rum, pineapple juice, tomato sauce, molasses, Worcestershire sauce, cider vinegar, dry mustard, olive oil, garlic, lime, and S&P in a small bowl and pour over the meat. Turn the chops or chicken over to coat completely. Marinate, covered, in the fridge for 2 hours or overnight, turning occasionally.

2 When you cook the meat, pour the sauce into a small saucepan, and bring to a boil over medium-high heat. Reduce heat and simmer, covered, on medium-low heat until sauce has reduced and thickened. Remove from heat, add butter, and stir to blend.

Did you know that pineapple is actually native to this continent? Most folks think of Hawaii when they think of this fruit, but actually it grows natively in the Caribbean and used to be grown in Florida as well. We visited Grandma in Florida, and somehow this ingredient made it onto her table in this sauce. I use it to marinate pork chops or chicken.

Serves 4

MINT MOJO

1 Combine all ingredients in a blender or processor. Blend until fairly smooth. Serve!

½ c mint

2 cl garlic, chopped roughly

2 T sugar

⅓ c red wine vinegar

⅓ c olive oil

S&P

★ ★

For a time, I really got into West Indies cooking and all the ingredients found there. Over time, I found my way back to the ingredients found on this continent and transformed some of the dishes I'd come to love, bringing them home. I make a batch of this sauce to accompany a platter of lamb pies, whip up a simple green salad, and call that an incredible meal. The sauce is tasty with smoked chicken, steak fingers, and pretty much anything you can imagine that would benefit from a tart-sweet mint sauce by its side.

STEAK RUB

3 T ground cinnamon

2 t brown sugar

1 t ground cumin

1 t paprika

½ t chili powder—any chili will do

½ t each S&P

½ t each ground nutmeg and cloves

Makes about ¼ cup

1 Combine spices in small bowl. Store, tightly covered, for up to 1 month. To use, sprinkle spice mixture evenly over meat or poultry, then rub the spices in with your fingers. Remember to wash your fingers well before touching anything else!

★ ★

It's the little touches that make a meal truly memorable. A rub of spice, a dip of sauce, a spoonful of relish—all these will have folks talking about "that thing you did" to dinner that they love so well. Here's a simple way to dress up a steak for dinner.

Serves 4–6

LEMON VINAIGRETTE

1 Mix garlic with salt, mustard, and lemon juice; whisk.

2 Drizzle in olive oil, whisking until thickened. Season with sugar, S&P.

Dressings aren't just for salads in our house. We always have one or two bottled in the fridge to go on just about anything that needs a little flavor added in. Steamed vegetables, soups, even a pile of chicken about to go on the grill can stand to benefit from a dash of this sauce thrown into the mix.

2 cl garlic, minced

½ t coarse salt

3 t Dijon mustard

4 T lemon juice

1 c olive oil

2 pinches sugar

S&P

BACON AND BLUE CHEESE VINAIGRETTE

Serves 4

8 oz. minced smoked bacon

3 shallots, minced

3 t thyme, chopped

4 T sherry vinegar

4 T olive oil

8 oz. blue cheese

1 In a small skillet render the bacon over medium heat until crispy.

2 Add the shallots and thyme and continue cooking for about 1 minute, then add the vinegar and olive oil.

3 Stir in the blue cheese and remove from the heat.

Here's another version of bacon in salad. This dressing can go on just about anything: chicken, burgers, green beans, let your imagination run wild!

HORSERADISH MAYONNAISE

Serves 4–6

1 Whisk the ingredients together in a small bowl.

½ c mayonnaise

2 T sour cream

3 T prepared horseradish

⅛ t freshly ground black pepper

¼ t salt

★ ★

This is an incredibly tasty option to top those sliders and is so easy to whip up at a moment's notice.

Vegetables

As a kid, one of my chores around the house was to tend to the kitchen garden. It was my job to thin seedlings, route out weeds, and apprise my mom when something was starting to come in so she could make preparations to turn whatever it was into something else. She sautéed, steamed, grilled, and performed magic in that kitchen. For months after the garden was turned under, we'd enjoy jars of whatever she'd canned up, bringing back the tastes of summer all winter long. I don't do much canning. I like to make something up and enjoy it right then and there. Here's my favorite recipes for veggies in all shapes and sizes, straight from the farmers' market to our table throughout the year.

SWEET AND SOUR CABBAGE

Serves 6

8 slices bacon

1 large head cabbage,
cored and shredded

¼ c flour

1 T caraway seed

S&P to taste

½ c white vinegar

½ c white sugar

1 Lay two slices of bacon across the bottom of a 12-inch Dutch oven. Cover with a layer of cabbage. Sprinkle a light dusting of flour and a pinch of caraway seed. Season with a little salt and pepper. Repeat layering as many times as possible until you run out of room.

2 Fill the pot with enough water to come about ¾ up the side. Bring to a boil, then reduce heat to medium and cook for about 45 minutes or until the cabbage is soft, stirring occasionally. Let cool slightly, then stir in the vinegar and sugar.

I worked on fishing boats in Alaska for a few years and, with all the Norwegians on board, came to love cooked cabbage, something I could never say before. Here's my version of a sweet and savory side dish that goes perfectly with pork chops and roasted potatoes—a fine way to hunker down in the winter. Plus, with the bacon in it, Jorge eats all his veggies up!

Serves 4

SAUTÉED GREENS

1 bunch greens, roughly chopped

2 T olive oil

½ onion, chopped

2–3 cl garlic, minced

½ t red pepper flakes

2 t bread crumbs

¼ c vinegar—white, sherry, whatever strikes your fancy

½ lemon, juiced

S&P to taste

1 Sauté garlic and onion in olive oil until soft. Add chopped greens and a dash of water to steam them slightly. Toss with onions and garlic and cook over medium heat about 4 minutes, until greens start to wilt.

2 Add vinegar, lemon, pepper flakes, bread crumbs, and S&P. Toss and cook over medium-low heat for another 3–4 minutes, until the flavors have combined well and the greens have clumped slightly, blackening in some spots while remaining wilted in others.

There are so many different ways to enjoy a nice pot of sautéed greens. I use whatever looks best and freshest at the market—mustard greens, kale, chard, beet greens, collard greens—you name it. What's truly great about this simple dish is that you can serve it as a side dish to accompany grilled just-about-anything, cornbread, and gingered beets or fold it into a pot of sausage ravioli along with a cup of stewed tomatoes to make a fine tossed pasta meal. Anyway you look at it, you're getting a whole heap of vitamins—and they taste great.

POTATO PANCAKES

Serves 4

6 med. potatoes

1 sm. onion

2 eggs

¼ c flour

½ t salt

Pinch baking powder

Pepper to taste

Vegetable oil

1 Grate potatoes in processor. Lay in a colander and place a bowl on top so that it fits neatly onto the potatoes. Press down to press out as much liquid as possible.

2 Chop or grate onion. Add to potatoes in processor along with everything except the oil. Process lightly or in short bursts until smooth yet slightly coarse.

3 Heat ⅛-inch oil in skillet until a drop of batter sizzles. Drop large spoonfuls into the skillet and, using the spoon, slightly flatten each spoonful to cook more evenly. Fry on both sides until brown and crisp, about 2–3 minutes on each side.

4 Drain on paper towels. Serve with sour cream and applesauce or anything you like.

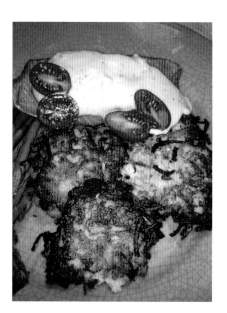

These are good anytime, covered in applesauce and sour cream for breakfast or alongside grilled sausages for dinner. I first made a batch of these when I was trying to make a breakfast hash and, tired from playing too late the night before (or is that waking up too early that day?), grated too many potatoes. I improvised, added a pinch of this and a spoonful of that, and here's what we ended up with. I know it's a lot like latkes but slightly different in that I make a batter out of the mix. Hopefully, you'll like them just the way they are.

WINTER VEGETABLES WITH CORNMEAL GRITS

Serves 4

1 Preheat oven to 500˚. Toss cauliflower, squash, and onion in large bowl with oil, garlic, ½ t pepper, salt, and nutmeg. Spread on baking sheet. Roast, turning once, until tender and browned in places, about 25–30 minutes.

2 Combine broth and water in small saucepan. Bring to boil over high heat. Reduce heat to low and slowly whisk in cornmeal, rosemary, and remaining pepper until smooth. Cover and cook, stirring occasionally, until very think and creamy, about 10–15 minutes. Stir in cheese and remove from heat. For additional flavor in the grits, add 2 T bacon grease before adding the cheese. Stir to blend, then add cheese.

3 Serve vegetables over grits.

We never get enough vegetables on the road. Often, we get home from tour, and I can feel my body craving vegetables, salad, and anything homemade. We'll sometimes go whole days just eating vegetables, although I often add a bit of bacon to appease Jorge. Here's one of my favorite comfort meals, rich and fulfilling enough to eat alone, or with a Mama's Day Steak. Try it!

4 c cauliflower florets

4 c cubed butternut squash

1 medium onion, sliced

2 T olive oil

2 cl garlic, minced

¾ t black pepper

¼ t salt

½ t nutmeg

2½ c broth—beef, chicken, or vegetable

1 c water

¾ c cornmeal

½ t dried rosemary

⅔ c cheddar cheese, grated

OKRA RELISH

Serves 4–6

1 c onion, chopped

3 cl garlic, chopped

1 T olive oil

2 c okra, chopped (10 oz. package frozen will do)

2 chilies, seeded and chopped

2 tomatoes, chopped

1 t salt

Pepper to taste

1 Sauté onions and garlic over medium heat until they turn soft, about 10 minutes. Add okra and chilies and sauté, stirring about 5 minutes.

2 Add tomatoes, salt, and pepper. Cover and simmer, stirring, for about 30 minutes, until flavors are all melded and you have a nice relish. Allow to cool before serving.

The first time I had okra, whoever had cooked it allowed the okra to turn slimy. Fatal error when feeding an 8-year-old. I hated the stuff, or so I thought, from that point on. Nanny, however, made up this relish to serve alongside hotdogs with mustard—and let me tell you, I found out I love okra after all!

Serves 4

STUFFED TOMATOES

1 Steam spinach for 4–5 minutes, then drain. Chop roughly and set aside.

2 In a large heavy skillet, sauté the onions, garlic, cinnamon, and paprika or chili powder in oil until onions are soft. Chop 2 tomatoes and add to the skillet with artichoke hearts, apple, and raisins. Cover and simmer on low heat until apple is soft, about 5–10 minutes. Add the spinach, almonds, and vinegar and simmer another 10 minutes, stirring occasionally. S&P to taste.

3 Preheat oven to 350˚. Halve and scoop out core of remaining tomatoes (or halve and remove inner rind from peppers) to leave ½–¾ inch of shell. Stuff filling in shells and place in buttered baking dish. Pour ½-inch water into dish to steam vegetables.

4 Bake covered 20 minutes. Remove cover and bake another 3–5 minutes more, until the vegetable mixture bubbles and turns slightly brown.

5 While the tomatoes are baking, puree all the nut sauce ingredients in a blender or processor until smooth. Warm on low heat in a small saucepan until the sauce is heated through. Serve tomatoes or peppers on a bed of rice with a healthy dollop of sauce on top.

6 medium firm tomatoes

10 oz. spinach, cleaned and stemmed

1 medium onion, chopped

1 cl garlic, chopped

¼ t cinnamon

¼ t paprika or chili powder

14 oz. can artichoke hearts, chopped

1 small apple, grated

⅓ c raisins

⅓ c finely chopped almonds

1 T vinegar

S&P to taste

3 T vegetable oil

SAUCE:

½ c sour cream

½ c pecans or walnuts, chopped

⅓ c cream cheese

½ c cheddar cheese, grated

1 t cinnamon

½ t paprika or chili powder

Come summer, when the garden is bursting at the seams, we come up with all sorts of ways to serve tomatoes, peppers, and anything else in abundance. Here's one way to serve tomatoes and peppers that makes a great side dish or main attraction alike.

Pictured page 76

CORN PUDDING

Serves 6

4 c cut corn

3 eggs

1/3 c melted butter

1/2 t salt

1/4 c sugar

1/2 c milk

1 T baking powder

1/4 t nutmeg

1/4 t allspice

1/4 c flour

1 Oil 9x5 baking dish. Preheat oven to 375˚.

2 In processor, puree 2 c corn with eggs, butter, salt, sugar, and milk until smooth.

3 In a mixing bowl, mix baking powder, nutmeg, allspice, and flour together. Add flour slowly to the wet mixture with processor on. When blended well, add remaining corn and pulse lightly to break it up a little to a coarse texture.

4 Pour batter into baking dish. Cover with foil and place inside another, larger baking dish. Pour hot water until it reaches halfway up the side of the corn pudding dish.

5 Bake 1½ hours until toothpick inserted into center of pudding comes out clean.

This is a wonderful warm savory pudding I started making a few years ago when I'd bit through my tongue and couldn't chew solid foods. Somehow I was still able to sing, though! It's also just a nice way to serve corn in the wintertime alongside a nice raisin glazed ham or pomegranate glazed turkey.

WINTER VEGETABLES WITH HORSERADISH

Serves 6–8

1 In mixing bowl, combine butter, oil, horseradish, vinegar, dill, and S&P. Add vegetables and toss to coat well. Spread out in roasting pan and bake at 475˚ for 35–40 minutes until vegetables are roasted through and browned.

2 If steaming, steam the vegetables first, then toss with the vinaigrette and serve.

★ ★

I love the heartwarming, belly-filling flavors of roasted winter vegetables. I came up with this recipe after rooting around in the fridge one evening to find something to do to them. Feel free simply to steam the vegetables too and then follow the recipe from there. Either way you serve them, you'll sigh when biting into the buttery yet vinegary-horseradish flavors.

1½ lbs. Brussels sprouts

3 carrots, cut into 1-inch slices

3 leeks, cut into 1-inch slices

2 Yukon Gold potatoes, cut into 1-inch-square cubes

2 T butter

⅓ c oil

3 T horseradish

3 T cider vinegar

1 T dill

S&P to taste

MAPLE GINGER BEETS

Serves 4

1 lb. beets, cut into ½-inch slices

¾ c water

1 t grated or minced fresh ginger or ½ t dried ground ginger

¼ t salt

3 T maple syrup

1 Place the beets, water, and ginger in a small saucepan and bring to a boil. Cover and cook over medium heat until the beets are tender, about 20–25 minutes.

2 Add the salt and maple syrup and continue to cook, uncovered, until the liquid is almost gone and the beets are shiny with the glaze.

As a child, I used to cut up beets and gnaw on them raw. I suppose it was the sugar I was after. I still go weak in the knees for this dish, combining the natural sweetness of beets with maple syrup and fresh ginger. This is the perfect foil for anything spicy or for simple fare, such as fried chicken.

Breaking Fast

Most musicians don't cotton much to the idea of rising too early. For some reason, though, I can't help it. Whenever we're on the road, I usually get first driving shift, as I'm usually the most awake. And at home I head into my office and write—or, if I'm really inspired, I'll whip up a batch of something delicious to surprise the "normal" musician still sleeping in the other room. Here's a selection of my own easy baked goods, hashes, and down-home scrambles that will give anyone a good kick-start for their day.

BLUEBERRY SCONES

Makes 8

2 c flour

2 t baking powder

½ t baking soda

¼ t salt

8 T cold butter, cut up into small cubes

¼ c sugar

1 egg

½ c blueberries

½ c buttermilk

1 Combine flour, baking powder, baking soda, salt, and sugar in bowl and mix well, then work butter into mixture until the texture resembles soft, coarse meal. Add blueberries and milk, mixing to make smooth but not sticky dough. If you need to add more flour to keep from sticking, then do so.

2 Roll dough to 1-inch height on lightly floured surface, keeping a circular shape. Cut circle into 8 wedges. Place the wedges, barely touching, on a baking pan. If you like, brush the tops with 1 beaten egg. Bake 20 minutes at 375° or until just browned.

When we're on tour, I don't eat much wheat since that affects my throat and singing. Once we're home, though, I rush to the oven and bake away, enjoying what I miss out on while on the road. These easy-to-make scones can also be made with strawberries, raspberries, or blackberries—any ripe berry will do.

APPLE FRITTERS

Serves 4–6

1 c flour

¼ c sugar

1 t salt

1½ t baking powder

⅓ c milk

1 egg

1 c finely chopped apple

Dash cinnamon

1 Sift flour, sugar, salt, baking powder, and cinnamon together. Add milk and egg. Beat to a smooth batter. Fold in apple.

2 Drop by spoonful into 2½–3-inch hot oil at about 375˚. Fry 2–3 minutes, turning over.

3 Drain on paper towels and gobble them up.

★ ★

Every year at Christmas, we used to drive up to Apple Hill to cut down a tree and gorge ourselves on hot apple cider and steaming apple fritters, fresh from the fryer. These are my own version, based on memories of those snowy, window-steamed, snap-cold days. Feel free to serve them hot with syrup or keep them in a container as a sweet snack for any time of the day.

CINNAMON APPLE RAISIN BREAD

Makes 1 loaf

2 c flour

1 c sugar

¼ t cinnamon

1½ t baking powder

½ t baking soda

½ t salt

1 c applesauce

2 eggs

½ c vegetable oil

¼ c milk

1 c raisins—dried apricots or prunes work well too

1 Grease loaf pan and set aside.

2 Mix flour, sugar, cinnamon, baking powder, baking soda, and salt well.

3 In another bowl, mix applesauce, eggs, oil, and milk.

4 Add wet mix to dry mix. Stir until smooth. Add dried fruit.

5 Pour batter into pan. Bake at 350˚ for 1 hour or until toothpick inserted into the center comes out clean.

6 Allow to cool 10 minutes before serving.

Another treat I like to make for the boys in the band is something baked before we head out onto the road. That way, after all the lamb pies and other treats are long gone, I can break out a well-hidden bag of home-baked bread or cookies to perk everyone up again. Sometimes I add a cup of fast-cooking oats to this recipe and cut the flour by half a cup to add another interesting texture to the mix.

Serves 2

CURRANT GRIDDLE CAKES

1 Combine flour, cornmeal, baking powder, spice, and salt in mixing bowl. Cut in butter and mix until it resembles a coarse meal. Add currants. Add just enough milk to make a piecrust-like dough, doughy but not too sticky.

2 Roll out onto lightly floured surface to ¼-inch thick. Cut into rounds 2 ½ inches in diameter. Or feel free to shape rough rounds directly from the mixing bowl, making sure to flatten them on a floured surface.

3 Coat heavy skillet with a small amount of oil. Fry cakes 4–5 minutes on each side over low heat until lightly browned. Keep finished cakes on a plate in the oven until all the cakes are fried up. Serve with syrup and fresh fruit.

1 c flour

¼ c corn meal

1 t baking powder

⅛ t salt

2 T butter

⅓ c currants

⅓–½ c milk

Pinch cinnamon, cardamom, allspice, whatever you like

Oil to fry

★ ★

One of the things I love about being a musician is when we get to stay with friends when we're out on tour. Normally, we stay in hotels, but every so often we have the luxury of sleeping in someone's home and waking up to a home-cooked meal. That's a soul-saver on the road. And when we return the favor, allowing musician friends to stay overnight with us, I often make a batch of these griddle cakes to start their late mornings out right.

CORNMEAL WAFFLES

Makes 16 waffles

3 c buttermilk

2 eggs

6 T melted butter

1 c rye flour

2 c cornmeal

2 t baking powder

1 t baking soda

¼ c sugar

2 t salt

1 Whisk together buttermilk, eggs, and butter in medium bowl. Combine dry ingredients in another bowl. Add the wet ingredients to the dry ingredients, gently mixing them together. Let batter rest for 10 minutes before using in your waffle press.

★ ★

There's something so satisfying about the earthy flavors of cornmeal and rye. For some reason, they both remind me of home. I make up a batch of whipped cream and sliced berries to go along with these waffles. Try them—you'll be hooked too.

Serves 2

KICKSTART HASH

1 Sauté potatoes in olive oil with 2 T water to help cook down for 8–10 minutes or until potatoes are soft and starting to brown at the edges. Add onion and garlic. Sauté until soft and the onions start to caramelize. Add sausage and sauté another 3–4 minutes.

2 Mix eggs with milk and seasonings in bowl. When eggs are well-blended, add to hash mix on stove. Cook until eggs are desired firmness, stirring often. Top with salsa on plate and serve with warmed tortillas or toast.

2 potatoes, shredded or cubed

1 T olive oil

¼ onion, diced

2 cl garlic, minced

1 sausage, cut into small cubes

4 eggs

¼ c milk, buttermilk, or cream

½ t Italian seasonings (basil, oregano, marjoram, thyme, rosemary)

We divvy up the chores in our house so that, when we're at home, everything runs as smoothly as possible. I handle all the shopping and cooking while Jorge takes care of the yard. Sometimes I help him out as a favor and, to repay my kindness, he asked me to teach him how to make breakfast for himself. Here's the one dish Jorge will cook up for you if you're ever touring through town and end up staying with us.

SNAKEHANDLERS MIGAS

Serves 2

²/₃ c crushed tortilla chips

½ onion, chopped

½ c tomato, diced

2 cl garlic, minced

½ c tomatillo, diced

2 t vegetable oil

1 c ground beef or pork—
2 sausages will do

4 eggs

¼ c milk, buttermilk, or cream

S&P

4 warmed corn tortillas

1 c cheddar cheese, grated

1 Sauté first 5 ingredients in oil over medium-high heat until onion is translucent, about 3–4 minutes. Add ground meat, stir to coat, and cook another 4–5 minutes, until the meat is sizzling and cooking through.

2 Whisk eggs with milk, S&P. Add to skillet, stirring until eggs reach desired firmness.

3 Spoon into warmed tortillas, top with cheese, and serve.

The first time we toured through Texas, we ate at this tiny Mexican café outside of San Antonio. The band was a bit weary that morning but feeling adventurous too. We all ordered migas, and a new house favorite was born. As soon as we got home from that tour, I started keeping the ingredients on hand to whip these up anytime, breakfast, lunch, or dinner! Sometimes I'll add pickled jalapeños or salsa to top the tortillas. Have fun coming up with your own variations.

Makes 1 11-in. pie

BREAKFAST PIE

¼ c butter

2 cl garlic, minced

1 sm. onion, chopped

1 can green chilies, chopped

4 tomatoes, chopped

1 jalapeño pepper, chopped

1 sausage, diced

6 eggs

1 c cheddar cheese, grated

S&P

½ t oregano

½ t cumin

Sour cream

PIE CRUST:

1¾ c flour

¾ t salt

9 T butter

4–5 T ice water

1 t chili powder

½ t cumin

1 In large bowl or processor, combine flour, salt, and herbs. Add butter in pats and work in with a fork or short bursts until the flour resembles a coarse meal. Sprinkle 4 tablespoons of water into the mix and stir firmly until dough shapes take form. Gather into a ball. Shape into a flat disk, about 6 inches in diameter. Roll out to ¼-inch thick on floured surface.

2 Line tart pan. Crimp edges with your thumb. Prick the dough with fork tines all over base of pan, about half an inch apart. Bake at 425˚ 10–15 minutes, until crust is dry and flaky but not browned. Let cool. Reduce heat to 375˚.

3 In large skillet, heat ½ butter and sauté onion and garlic until soft. Add sausage and cook 3–4 minutes, until sausage is lightly browned. Add chilies, tomato, and jalapeño and sauté 3 minutes more, until tomato starts to soften. Transfer to a mixing bowl and set aside.

4 Add remaining butter, pour in eggs, and sprinkle with cheese. Soft scramble the eggs, adding S&P and spices. Gently stir in tomato mixture and cook another minute or two until eggs are cooked all the way through.

5 Spoon into the tart shell. Bake at 375˚ for 5–10 minutes to set. Remove and let settle for a few minutes before serving. Garnish with sour cream and salsa if you like.

★ ★

Here's another version of migas, only served up in a nice self-contained pie. Basically, any chance I get to bake, I do. This pie was an experiment I set for myself, wondering whether anything I could dream up I could also bake. The answer is yes. Add cut-up pieces of broccoli, leeks, squash, you name it, to come up with your own version of a breakfast pie or enjoy this version too!

MINTED FRUIT SALAD

1 papaya or mango, peeled and diced

1 c strawberries, halved or quartered

2 c melon of any kind, diced

1 banana, cut into ½-inch slices

2 oranges, peeled, with segments
cut into halves

2 kiwis, diced

¼ c fresh mint

3 T sugar

1 cup raspberries or blueberries

Serves 4

1 Place all fruit except raspberries/
blueberries in a mixing bowl.

2 Process sugar and mint until well
ground and blended. Add to fruit.

3 Add berries and toss everything
lightly to coat with mint-sugar mix.
Set aside for 10 minutes and serve.

I like a bowl of fruit salad as much as almost anyone. When we're on the
road, we don't get much fresh fruit, so I dream about it, honestly. Here's
my own slightly sweetened version, dressed up with a hint of mint for
fun. If you're having this for dessert, mix a few tablespoons of Grand
Marnier with another few tablespoons of honey and drizzle over the
salad just before serving. That's truly tasty.

Meats

As Americana as anything, recipes that call for some type of meat hearken back to before Columbus. Native people hunted bison, buffalo, and deer. And early on, the Spanish and English brought over cattle, goats, sheep, and pigs, which were all added to the menu. I grew up on a farm that raised cattle, and there was always a neighbor who'd just slaughtered a pig or sheep somewhere nearby. These recipes are a combination of good-old-boy BBQ and farmhouse kitchen dishes handed down for generations, as well as a handful of recipes I've put together myself over the years. Whenever we have guests over for special celebrations, I make sure to make up one of these beloved dishes so that they feel they've been fed right.

BLUE CHEESE, PECAN, APPLE-STUFFED BACON-WRAPPED PORK CHOPS

Serves 2

2 boneless pork chops, butterflied

4 oz. crumbled blue cheese

2 slices bacon

½ apple, chopped

3 oz. pecans, chopped

S&P to taste

½ c white wine or other liquor

½ c broth—chicken or vegetable

1 T butter

1 Preheat the oven to 325˚. Grease a shallow baking dish.

2 Season each chop with S&P. In a small skillet, sear both pork chops over medium-high heat for a few minutes on each side, to brown.

3 In a small bowl, mix together blue cheese, pecans, and apples. Stuff half into each pork chop. Wrap one slice bacon around each chop and secure with a toothpick.

4 Place chops in baking dish. Add additional apple slices, potatoes, turnips, and any autumn produce you feel like roasting to the dish. Bake for 40 minutes, turning over once, until the chops are done to your desired degree of doneness.

5 Meanwhile, deglaze the skillet with wine or other liquor. Add broth and butter and cook over medium heat until it reduces by half for a thick sauce. Pour over pork chops and roasted vegetables to serve.

Sure, it's a mouthful to say and oh-so-much more of a mouthful to enjoy. This is a rich recipe I made up to enjoy the well-matched flavors of apple, blue cheese, pecans, and bacon, all wrapped up in a hearty main dish. Serve with potato pancakes and sautéed greens and you'll be singing soon enough.

Serves 6–8

WILD GAME SWEET CHILI

1 Brown meat in Dutch oven. Add beans, onion, garlic, bacon, and S&P. Pour beer and enough water to cover beans. Cover and simmer 1–2 hours until the beans are tender.

2 Add tomatoes, jalapeño, and seasonings. Continue to simmer another hour or until flavors have melded nicely.

3 Serve with a dollop of sour cream on top and a healthy wedge of corn bread on the side.

★ ★

A few years back, a friend and I drove across Idaho and Montana, stopping at every back road meat and produce stand along the way. We picked up a bunch of wild boar bacon and freshly ground bison and, after rifling through what we'd brought along with us for the trip, came up with this sweet and spicy version of campfire chili to enjoy anytime, anywhere. The trick is to use a heavy Dutch oven, whether you cook this over coals or in your kitchen at home. There's something about a nicely seasoned iron pot that brings out all the good flavors in this dish.

1 lb. ground meat—bison, buffalo, deer, you name it

6 c dry beans

2 onions, chopped

8 cl garlic, minced

1 lb. bacon, chopped

2 t salt

1 t black pepper

1 beer

2 No. 2 cans tomatoes

½ jalapeño

½ c honey

1 c brown sugar

6 T maple syrup

2 t cinnamon

1 t ea. cloves and allspice

2 T chili powder

1–2 t Tabasco

¼ c Worcestershire sauce

VENISON STEW

Serves 4–6

4 slices bacon, chopped

3 lbs. venison, cut into 1-inch cubes

2–3 c red wine

¾ onion, chopped

½ lb. mushrooms , sliced

½ lb. carrots, chopped

½ lb. potatoes, chopped

2 leeks, chopped

10 oz. broth—beef or vegetable

1 T tomato paste

S&P to taste

½ t thyme

Bay leaf

2 cl garlic, minced

1 T parsley

1 Fry bacon in Dutch oven until crisp. Set aside. Brown venison. Set aside with bacon. Deglaze Dutch oven with ¼ c wine. Add onions and mushrooms with butter and cook until onions are slightly caramelized and browned. Add carrots, potatoes, and leeks and cook until vegetables are soft.

2 Add broth, tomato paste, S&P, thyme, bay leaf, garlic, and parsley Add meats back to pot along with butter and remaining wine. Simmer, covered, until the flavors meld together, about 15 minutes longer.

3 You can add peas, Tabasco, paprika, or just about any other details you like to this stew. You almost can't go wrong!

This is another hearty, savory dish we enjoyed while out on the road once or twice. We'd have our stack of Dutch ovens cooking away over coals, and other campers would walk by and gawk a little. Sometimes, to be neighborly, we'd carry a freshly cooked-up Dutch oven crumble coffee cake around to the other campsites and share. There's nothing like a belly full of good hearty stew to make you feel neighborly.

Serves 4

MEAT LOAF

1 Preheat oven to 350˚.

2 Combine all ingredients in a bowl and mix well.

3 Shape into loaf in an oiled loaf pan. Top with a few tablespoons of homemade BBQ sauce if you like.

4 Bake, uncovered, 1–1¼ hours, until crusty and browned on top and cooked all the way through.

What's more Americana than a savory slice of meatloaf, topped with gravy and served up with a hearty helping of mashed potatoes and peas? Well, there's a lot of ways you could answer that question, but the one I'm looking for is "nearly nothing." This meal reminds me of home more than almost anything. Whenever we tour Europe, we'll often talk about the meals I'm going to prepare once we're home again, and this is nearly always at the top of the list.

1½ lbs. ground beef

1 c milk

1 T Worcestershire sauce

¼ t ea. sage and thyme

½ t salt

½ t mustard

¼ t pepper

2 cl garlic, minced

1 small onion, chopped

½ c bread crumbs

½ c catsup

1 egg

MAMA'S DAY STEAK

Serves 4

4 8oz. steaks—top loin or tenderloin

2 t black pepper

Salt

1 c crumbled blue cheese

CHOCOLATE BALSAMIC SAUCE

1 c balsamic vinegar

2 T chocolate syrup

2 T butter

1 Sprinkle steaks with pepper and salt. Grill steaks to desired doneness. The last 3 minutes, sprinkle blue cheese on top.

2 In small saucepan combine vinegar and chocolate sauce. Bring to boil, reduce heat, and simmer 10 minutes until reduced by half. Remove from heat and add butter.

3 Drizzle sauce over steaks and serve with mashed potatoes or stuffed tomatoes.

I made up this delicious recipe to honor my own mother on the real Mother's Day—that is, my birthday. For years, every year, I'd call up Mom and tell her "Happy Mother's Day," then cook this meal in her honor, as I did the very first time I made it for her. The delicate taste of balsamic vinegar blends so enticingly with chocolate and blue cheese, Mom's favorites.

Serves 4

PAPA'S DAY STEAK

1 Sauté shallots in 1 t oil over medium-high heat until they begin to brown, about 15–20 minutes. Remove shallots from pan and set aside.

2 Combine thyme with S&P in a small bowl. Rub mixture all over steaks. Add remaining oil to skillet and cook steaks 5–7 minutes per side or to desired doneness. Transfer to plate, tent, and keep warm in warmed oven.

3 Add Madeira to pan and cook for 1 minute. Add broth and bring to a boil. Continue cooking until the liquid has reduced by half, about 10–12 minutes.

4 Combine flour and butter in small bowl. Stir tomato paste into skillet until dissolved, then add flour-butter mixture. Mix well until dissolved. Add prunes and continue cooking until sauce has thickened, about 2–3 minutes more. Add shallots and steaks back into pan, turning to coat everything evenly. Cook about 1–2 minutes longer. Serve the steaks smothered in the pan sauce along with corn pudding or whatever pleases.

4 4-oz. sirloin steaks

5 shallots, sliced

3 t olive oil

1 T thyme

½ t ea. salt and pepper

¾ c Madeira

14 oz. broth—beef or vegetable

1 t flour

1 t soft butter

1 t tomato paste

¼ c pitted prunes, chopped

I couldn't very well create a dish for Mom and not make something up for Papa too. Well, it's actually Jorge's favorite, but we'll just say "Papa" to make all things fair and square. The sauce is maddeningly addictive—enjoy...

LAMB BURGERS

Serves 4

2 T currants

2 T pine nuts

1 t parsley

1 t mint

1 t lemon zest and 1 t lemon juice

2 cl garlic, chopped

S&P to taste

½ t ea. cumin, curry powder, cinnamon

1½ lbs. lamb, ground

1 Place currants, pine nuts, parsley, mint, lemon, garlic, and S&P in a processor and process in short bursts until you form a loose paste.

2 Place lamb in a mixing bowl and add paste and remaining spices. Blend well by hand until all ingredients are well meshed.

3 Form patties and grill over medium-hot fire for about 5 minutes on each side or until desired doneness.

I'd purchased some lamb to make a delicious lamb stew with apricots, garlic, and carrots, when some friends called and invited us to an impromptu BBQ at their home. I ground the lamb up and added a bit of this and that until I felt we had something worth throwing on the grill. The burgers turned out to be incredibly tasty—I even had to write the recipe out for a few folks at the party—so now we make them about once a month. I serve them with a spoonful of onion or okra relish and a dab of mayonnaise and mustard on warmed corn tortillas.

BABY BACK RIBS WITH APRICOT BBQ SAUCE

Serves 4

1 In a large pot, combine ribs with onion, garlic, bay leaves, and cumin. Add water to cover and bring to a boil over high heat for 5 minutes. Drain and rinse the ribs well. Save the onions and set aside.

2 Combine all BBQ sauce ingredients in a heavy saucepan. Simmer until the sauce has thickened and flavors have melded, about 6–7 minutes.

3 Preheat oven to 250˚. Place the onions in the bottom of a roasting pan. Add water to a depth of 1 inch. Place roasting rack on top, brushed with oil. Sprinkle the ribs with lime juice, S&P, and brush on both sides with BBQ sauce. Tent the pan and bake ribs until very tender, about 2 hours.

4 Just before serving, grill ribs until crusty and brown, about 2–3 minutes per side. Brush with remaining BBQ sauce.

3 lbs. baby back ribs

1 onion, quartered

2 bay leaves

1 t cumin

2 cl garlic

SAUCE:

1 c apricot jam

1 T soy sauce

6 T cider vinegar

2 t catsup

¼ c bourbon

2 t Worcestershire sauce

¼ c tomato paste

2 T onion, minced

¼ c lime juice

1 t ginger, ground

2 cl garlic, minced

½ hot chili, minced

S&P to taste

At one of my restaurants some years ago, one of my chefs created a stellar rib dish that had me eating way too many ribs way too often. He hailed from a family that could claim many tribes—with a bit of Seminole, some Louisiana Creole, African American, Irish, you name it—he had a touch of that blood in his. His cooking reflected his heritage, and this recipe showcases it best. I changed the recipe a bit to reflect my own heritage—and hope you like it as much as I do.

BEER GLAZED RIBS

Serves 4

2 lbs. pork loin ribs

12 oz. bottle stout or other dark beer

½ c onion, chopped

¼ c prepared mustard—I like whole grain, but any will do

2 T brown sugar

3 cl garlic, minced

1 t caraway seeds

S&P to taste

1 Mix beer, onion, mustard, brown sugar, garlic, and caraway in a large mixing bowl. Add ribs, toss to coat with marinade. Cover and refrigerate for 6 hours or overnight, making sure to turn the ribs occasionally. Drain, reserving marinade.

2 Sprinkle ribs with S&P. Pour marinade into small saucepan. Bring to a boil, then reduce heat and simmer, uncovered, about 15 minutes until sauce is reduced by half.

3 Place ribs on a lightly oiled grill rack over medium heat. Cover and grill for about 40–45 minutes or until juices run clear, turning the ribs every 15 minutes or so. Brush the ribs often with the reduced sauce during the last 10 minutes of grilling. Serve with corn pudding and fried dill pickles.

I know there's a lot of fuss over what "true" BBQ really is: smoked, or not, served smothered in sauce, or not, served spicy, or not. There are all kinds of BBQ for all kinds of people in this large and lovely country of ours. Here's my personal take on a true-blue Americana favorite. Make sure you listen to anything with some good banjo playing while you cook these up.

PINEAPPLE RUM BBQ SHORT RIBS

Serves 6

1 Combine brown sugar, paprika, garlic, pepper, salt, and cumin together in bowl. Rub onto ribs. Cover and chill for 2–4 hours.

2 Place ribs in a large pot just covered with water and bring to a boil. Reduce heat and simmer, uncovered, for about 1½ hours, or until tender.

3 Prepare pineapple rum sauce (pg 70).

4 Grill ribs on lightly oiled grill rack about 15 minutes over medium heat or until tender. Brush occasionally with sauce as you grill. Serve with garlic mashed potatoes, corn bread, and okra relish—mm-mm good.

4 T brown sugar

2–4 t paprika

3 cl garlic, minced

6 t black pepper

3 t salt

1 t cumin

6 lbs. beef short ribs

The first time we played in Memphis, we were fed some of the finest short ribs I'd ever tasted. Now, while I don't claim to cook up BBQ Memphis-style, here's my take on the ribs we ate that day. Serve them up with a hearty pile of sweet potatoes or spicy onion rings and a frosty glass of something thirst-quenching!

COCA COLA BABY BACK RIBS

Serves 6

4 lbs. baby back ribs

1 liter bottle of Coca-Cola

1 large onion, quartered

1 cl garlic, chopped

2 bay leaves

1 T whole black peppercorns

SAUCE

1 stick butter

1 small white onion diced

1 cl garlic, minced

1 c catsup

1 T Dijon mustard

¼ c brown sugar

1 t Worcestershire sauce

12 oz. can Coca-Cola

1 Mix the liter bottle of Coca-Cola, onion, garlic, bay leaves, and peppercorns in a large pot. Add the ribs and, if necessary, a bit of water just to ensure the ribs are completely covered. Bring to a boil and reduce heat to a simmer, turning the ribs occasionally, until the meat pulls away from the bone, about 1 hour.

2 Meanwhile, combine the butter, onion, garlic, catsup, mustard, brown sugar, Worcestershire sauce, and 12 oz. Coca-Cola in large heavy sauce pan. Bring to a boil and reduce heat. Simmer for about 25 minutes, stirring often until sauce is thickened and reduced. Season to taste with S&P and let cool slightly. Using a blender or processor, puree the sauce.

3 Remove the ribs from the pot, pat dry, season with S&P, and brush liberally with the sauce. Grill, turning often, until charred on the outside, about 8 minutes, over medium-high heat. Loosely tent the ribs with foil and let rest for 5 minutes before cutting into individual ribs. Serve extra sauce on the side along with stuffed tomatoes and sweet potato fries.

Just about the best thing my mom ever made was these ribs, never often enough for my liking, though. Here's her recipe, more or less—I always change things to suit my particular taste preferences and urge you to do so too. Have fun eating these!

Poultry

We used to raise chickens, and once a neighbor brought over a dozen live wild turkeys as a gift. We penned them and fed them for a while—but danged if those birds aren't sorta stupid! Remind me to tell you stories sometime when you catch us on tour. We got creative with recipes involving those dumb birds. Over the years, I've had many opportunities to cook up pheasant, quail, pigeon, partridge, and duck. Here are some of my favorite recipes that have been tested out over time, much to the delight of friends and family.

APPLE ROASTED QUAIL

Serves 2

2–3 quail

1 carrot

1 apple

1 onion

1 t thyme

S&P

2 bacon strips per quail

2 c broth—chicken or vegetable

1 c applesauce

1 c maple syrup

1 Chop carrot, apple, and onion roughly and mix together with thyme.

2 S&P quail cavities. Stuff with apple-carrot-onion mix. Place birds in Dutch oven and lay 2 pieces of bacon atop each bird. Add broth to pot.

3 Cover and cook 3 hours at 275˚ or until tender. Remove Dutch oven from heat. Drain liquid. Replace quail in Dutch oven and roast until browned. Meanwhile, in a small bowl mix applesauce and maple syrup. Brush onto quail and cook 20–30 minutes longer, until well-glazed and brown. Serve with potato-apple bake and soda bread.

A close friend of mine goes bird hunting every year. Lucky for me, he brings back some of what he bags for me to cook up—sort of a win-win situation for both of us. I get to enjoy these luscious birds, and he gets to dine on something scrumptious. Once again, I turn to the quintessential Americana cooking method—in a Dutch oven over coals—and make sure to surround the bird with local Americana flavors.

Serves 4

SMOKED CHICKEN

10–20 pieces of chicken: thighs, legs, or breasts cut into 2-in. pieces

1 c brown sugar

1 c black tea

Sesame seeds

MARINADE:

3 cl garlic, minced

1 T ginger

1 T honey

¾ c soy sauce

½ c sherry

1 Mix garlic, ginger, honey, soy sauce, and sherry in a bowl. Add chicken and toss to coat well. Marinate at least 2 hours, turning every so often.

2 Line the bottom of a Dutch oven with foil and sprinkle sugar and tea there. Place a wire rack over sugar-tea mixture and arrange chicken on top.

3 Cook on medium-high, covered, for 30 minutes. Turn the heat off but keep the cover on the pot for 20 minutes to allow the smoke to settle into the bird.

4 When ready to serve, remove the chicken and sprinkle with sesame seeds. Enjoy with a side of wild rice and sautéed greens.

On a tour that took us through San Francisco years ago, I picked up a curious block of tea in Chinatown. By the time we got home, the block had broken apart, and I found myself with all this tea. I had to do something. I remembered seeing rows of tea-smoked ducks in one of the Chinatown butcher shops and came up with this easy-to-make-at-home recipe. And, yes, I used up all that tea. You will want either to cook this outside or have your fan on high, as the tea mixture really smokes.

FIESTA-STUFFED CHICKEN

Serves 4

4 chicken breasts

¾ t chili powder

¾ t cumin

½ t salt

¼ t paprika

½ c bread crumbs

2 T butter

¼ c celery, chopped

¼ c onion, chopped

½ c corn

¼ c cheddar cheese, shredded

2 T cilantro, chopped

1 Butter 12x8 baking dish. In small bowl, combine chili powder, cumin, salt, and paprika. Reserve 1 t of mixture and set aside. To remaining mixture, add breadcrumbs and mix well.

2 In medium skillet, melt butter. Add celery and onions. Cook 5–7 minutes until vegetables are tender. Add corn, cheese, cilantro, and breadcrumb mixture. Mix well.

3 Loosen skin from each chicken breast to form pocket between skin and meat. Fill each pocket with ¼ of the corn mixture. Secure opening with toothpick if need be.

4 Return chicken to skillet and cook over medium-high heat until browned on outside, about 4–5 minutes, turning once.

5 Place chicken, skin side up, in baking dish. Sprinkle chicken with reserved seasoning mixture and bake at 350˚ about 35–40 minutes, until juices run clear.

As a nod to our neighbors to the south, I often use some of the best-loved ingredients found in Central Texas grocery stores. I came up with this recipe when we ran out of propane one day and I was forced to throw the chicken into the oven. Baking it actually allowed the chicken to retain its moisture and sealed all the flavors together really nicely.

POMEGRANATE GLAZED TURKEY

Serves 4

4 turkey cutlets, about 1 lb.

4 fennel bulbs, sliced

5 t vegetable oil

½ t thyme

1 t salt

¾ t pepper

1 c pomegranate juice

¼ c broth—chicken or vegetable

1 t flour

1 T butter

1 Preheat oven to 450°. Toss fennel, 3 t oil, thyme, and ¼ t ea. S&P in a medium bowl. Spread onto a baking sheet. Roast in oven, stirring once or twice, until golden and tender, about 25 minutes.

2 Sprinkle both sides of turkey with remaining salt and pepper. Heat remaining oil in skillet over medium-high heat. Add turkey and cook until browned, 2–3 minutes per side. Remove turkey to a plate.

3 Add pomegranate juice to pan. Bring to a boil, stirring often, until reduced to ¼ c, about 7–10 minutes. Whisk together broth, flour, and butter to break up lumps. Add to the pan and cook, stirring constantly until thickened, about 1–2 minutes.

4 Reduce heat to medium, return the turkey and fennel mixture to the pan, turning to coat well, and cook for 1–2 minutes. Serve with horseradish mashed potatoes and pecan green beans.

The pomegranate first reached America via El Conquistadores. When I was a child, some neighbors of ours had a pomegranate tree, and the son would sometimes tuck a few of the round, juicy red fruits into his shirt to bring them over to us. We lived across a highway from these neighbors, and once the son got hit by a car on his way over to our place. He was fine—a little bruised—but the pomegranates broke inside his shirt, and we all thought he was a goner. The next time he brought fruit over for us, my mom made up a batch of chicken in pomegranate as a sort of "thank you/get well" card. Here's my version of that dish.

FRIED CHICKEN

Serves 4–6

3–4 lbs. chicken, cut up

DREDGE:

4 c flour

1 t garlic powder

1 t onion powder

½ t cayenne

DRENCH:

2 c white wine

1 egg

1 T Worcestershire sauce

1 t salt

hot sauce to taste

S&P to taste

Oil to fry, with a little bacon grease

1 Mix dredge ingredients. Mix drench ingredients. Heat oil to medium-high heat.

2 First drench, then dredge the chicken pieces, turning to evenly coat with all ingredients.

3 Fry both sides until brown, about 10 minutes on each side. You may need to add oil as you go along, depending on how large your skillet is—i.e., how many pieces of chicken you can fry at once. Once your oil turns golden brown, it will start to color and flavor the chicken faster than before, although the cooking time will remain the same. So, later fried pieces in older oil will turn out darker and more heavily oil-flavored than those fried in cleaner, newer oil.

There is a wealth of fried food in the south, fried chicken being one of the most commonly found specialty dishes everywhere you go. Some like it a little crispier, some with a thinner crust, some with some spice, and some just barely fried at all. This recipe reminds me of dinner at Nanny and Pappaw's. Make sure to serve it up with some homemade biscuits and gravy to enjoy it all just the way Nanny made it.

Serves 4

PECAN CHICKEN

4 boneless, skinless chicken breasts

¼ t cayenne

½ c pecans

¼ c bread crumbs

1½ t grated orange zest

½ t salt

1 egg white

1 T oil

1 Pound chicken between 2 sheets of plastic wrap until ¼-inch thick.

2 Process pecans, bread crumbs, zest, cayenne, and salt in blender or processor until finely ground. Transfer to a bowl.

3 Whisk egg and 2 T water together. Dip chicken in the egg, then into the dry mix.

4 Heat oil to medium heat and cook chicken on both sides about 3–5 minutes, until nicely browned and cooked through. Serve with a huge helping of mac 'n' cheese, sautéed greens, and pecan cornbread. Make your friend smile again.

A friend was going through a difficult time some years ago. We invited her over for dinner and some music to cheer her up. I made all the best comfort foods I could think of, and by the time she left at the end of that night, well-stuffed to the gills, she had a big smile on her face that lasted all week long. Next time you or a friend are having a hard time, try this recipe on for size.

LEMON BAKED CHICKEN

Serves 4

5 T butter

¼ c parsley

1 T grated lemon peel

3 cl garlic, minced

2 T lemon juice

2 lemons, cut into quarters

16 oz. artichoke hearts

2 lbs. White Rose potatoes

5 lbs. chicken, whole

S&P to taste

1 Preheat oven to 425˚. Mix butter, parsley, lemon peel, garlic, and S&P to taste together.

2 Loosen skin around breast area on chicken and spread 2 T lemon mixture under skin and 1 T over on each side. Sprinkle with S&P. Stuff lemon quarters inside the chicken's cavity.

3 Roast 45 minutes in heavy baking dish. Arrange artichokes, potatoes, and any extra lemons around the bird. Roast, basting every so often, another 25 minutes, or until nicely browned and done.

4 Serve with winter vegetables with horseradish or maple gingered beets.

Over the last few years, whenever I visit home, my brother and I cook for Mom. It's only fair, as long as she makes up a batch of homemade fudge to sweeten the deal. Here's one of the first meals I made on a trip home, based on a picture I saw in a cooking magazine. We couldn't find the recipe, but I pored over that picture and came up with this recipe!

Serves 4

ISLAND CHICKEN

1 Sprinkle S&P and ¼ t ginger over chicken. Cook in medium-sized skillet over medium heat about 10–12 minutes, turning to cook evenly. Remove from skillet.

2 Add fruit to skillet and cook until slightly soft. Add ½ c water, vinegar, and sugar and cook for another minute or so. Add coconut and remaining ginger. Stir well to blend. Add chicken back into skillet to warm through. Serve with white rice and any sort of fresh, steamed vegetables.

4 chicken breasts, cut into ¾-inch wide strips

½ t ground ginger

1 T olive oil

½ c dried cherries

1 apple, thinly sliced

⅓ c coconut

4 t brown sugar

3 T cider vinegar

S&P to taste

One of my fondest memories as a child is pulling into some roadside diner somewhere and being served a fine dish of cherries, coconut, and Coca-Cola in a sort of Jell-O-like dessert. I took those same flavors and turned them into a savory-sweet main dish so I don't feel so guilty every time I make it.

PEACHY CHICKEN

3–4 lbs., chicken, cut up

⅓ c white wine

⅓ c brandy

½ apple, sliced

1 lb. peaches, sliced

DREDGE:

2 t salt

1 c flour

¼ t cayenne

½ t garlic powder

½ t onion powder

Serves 4

1 Combine dredge ingredients. Toss pieces of chicken in dredge to coat.

2 Heat ½ inch oil in pan to medium heat. Add chicken and cook until brown on both sides, turning, about 7–10 minutes. Add apple, peaches, and wine. Cook, covered, for 20 minutes. Turn chicken over and add brandy. Boil, reduce heat, and simmer, covered, for another 20 minutes.

3 Serve with sautéed greens, spiced onion rings, and hush puppies to soak up the sauce.

Every year, Nanny would send us home with a few highly coveted jars of apricot preserves. We would dole them out carefully over the next year so as not to run out. This recipe reminds me of Nanny, through and through, every time I make it.

Mushroom Stroganoff

Serves 4

WILD MUSHROOM CHICKEN STROGANOFF

1 In a medium-sized heavy skillet, cook onion in oil over high heat until the onion starts to turn translucent, about 2–3 minutes. Add chicken and cook another 4–5 minutes. Add ½ t salt, mushrooms, black pepper, cayenne, and soy sauce. Continue cooking over high heat, stirring occasionally, until the liquid has gone and the mushrooms are seared to a lovely brown.

2 Reduce heat to medium and add thyme, basil, and sherry. Simmer until the sherry is reduced by half, about 5–10 minutes. Remove from the heat.

3 Add sour cream, parsley, and tarragon. Stir to blend. Set aside.

4 Meanwhile, bring a large pot of water to a boil. Add ¼ t salt. Add fettuccine and cook until just soft and cooked through. Drain the pasta in a colander. Transfer to a plate and top with the mushroom-chicken mixture. Serve with love.

4 chicken breasts, cut into ¾-inch thick strips

1 yellow onion, chopped

1 T olive oil

1 lb. wild mushrooms—morels, chanterelles, porcini, any and all will do

½ t salt

¼ t black pepper

Cayenne to taste

1 T soy sauce

¼ t thyme

½ t basil

⅓ c dry sherry or Marsala wine

1 c sour cream

2 t parsley

1 T tarragon

8–10 oz. dried fettuccine

★ ★

A friend of mine goes mushrooming every year. He has his own special private patch that he'll tell no one about, where he goes throughout the season to harvest lovely wild mushrooms of all types. He taught me not to cook these wild flavors too heavily, but rather to let them stand up and speak for themselves in any dish. Here's one of my favorite ways of enjoying the wonderful flavors wild mushrooms bring to the table.

CHICKEN POT PIE

Serves 4

CRUST:

1½ c flour

½ c chilled butter

3 T ice water

½ t salt

ROUX:

2 T butter

2 T flour

1 c sour cream, yogurt, or buttermilk

¼ t nutmeg

1 T Dijon mustard

2 c cheddar cheese, grated

TOPPING:

1 T butter

⅔ c bread crumbs

¼ t ea. marjoram and basil

Dash paprika

FILLING:

3 T olive oil

1 onion, chopped

2 carrots, diced

1 Yellow Finn potato, diced

4 chicken breasts, cut into 1-inch pieces

½ t ea. Hungarian paprika, basil, and marjoram

½ c diced bell pepper

1 c mushrooms, sliced

½ c green peas

½ c corn

Nanny once told me that you can make just about anything into a pie. Yankees and southerners alike have been known to cook two or three different types of pie for every meal. There was a time when you would easily find meat pies, fruit pies, vinegar pies, custard pies—both savory and sweet—and the list goes on, to cover everything from main courses to side dishes and desserts alike. This is a wonderfully belly-warming winter main dish sort of pie. It can easily be served all on its own.

1 Sift flour and salt in mixing bowl. Cut in butter, using your fingertips until the mixture resembles a coarse meal. Sprinkle ice water over the mixture, a little at a time, as you turn the dough until a ball forms. Chill until firm, about 45–60 minutes, or immediately roll out to ¼ inch on a lightly floured surface. Place the dough into a 9x11 baking dish and set aside.

2 In a large saucepan sauté the onions until soft. Add carrots, potatoes, chicken, paprika, basil, and marjoram. Cook, covered, on medium heat, stirring often, about 10 minutes. Add the bell pepper, mushrooms, peas, and corn. S&P to taste. Cover and continue to cook until the carrots start to become tender, about 7–10 minutes.

3 In another saucepan, make the roux. Melt the butter, add flour, and stir constantly on low heat for 3–5 minutes. When the flour starts to brown, whisk in the sour cream, mustard, and nutmeg. Continue to cook over low heat, stirring, until lightly thickened. Add the grated cheese and stir in until well-blended. Remove from heat.

4 In a small skillet, make the topping. Melt the butter on low heat. Add the breadcrumbs and herbs, stir to coat them in the butter, and sauté for about 3–4 minutes or until the breadcrumbs begin to brown.

5 Assemble the pie. Spoon the vegetables and chicken into the piecrust. Pour the roux over the filling. Sprinkle on the breadcrumbs. Bake for 40 minutes at 375˚.

Fish & Seafood

We have so many coastlines along the "edges" of our great big, beautiful country that it's easy to find a plethora of local, home-style regional dishes boasting all different flavors of life. Here's a collection of our personal favorites, from northeast oyster bisques to northwest smoked salmon, southwest baked seafood, to southern sour orange tuna. You'll find a lot of great flavors to match nearly any mood you're in for seafood.

OYSTER BISQUE TART

Makes 1 11-in. pie

18 large oysters, or 24–30 small

1 leek, chopped

1 carrot, chopped

4 shallots, minced

¼ c cognac or brandy

1 T fresh parsley

¼ t ea. dry thyme and tarragon

S&P to taste

2 eggs

½ c half and half

2 T butter

DOUGH:

1 c flour + 6 T

½ c cornmeal

½ t salt

8 T butter, cold

4–5 T ice water

1 Combine flour, cornmeal, and salt in processor or bowl. Add butter in pats and cut in until consistency resembles coarse meal. Sprinkle water, a little at a time, over mixture and process in short bursts or mix by hand until small clumps form. Gather clumps into ball. Shape into flat disk, about 6 inches in diameter. Roll or pat out to ¼-inch thick on lightly floured surface. Line tart pan and crimp edges with thumb. Prick with fork tines all over the bottom of tart, about half an inch apart. Bake 10–15 minutes at 425˚. Crust should be flaky but not quite browned. Reduce oven temp to 375˚ and set the crust aside.

2 In a large skillet, melt butter and sauté shallots, carrots, and leeks until soft and slightly browned.

3 Add oysters, cognac, herbs, and S&P. Sauté over medium heat until oysters are plumped and cooked through and liquid has evaporated.

4 Whisk together eggs and half and half to make custard. Spoon 1 tablespoon hot oyster mix into custard to warm. Then stir custard into oyster mixture. Spread into prepared tart shell.

5 Bake in lower third of oven about 25 minutes at 375˚, until custard is set and a toothpick inserted into the middle comes out clean. Allow to set on a rack for about 15 minutes before serving. Serve with stuffed tomatoes.

★ ★

This recipe reminds me of the first time I sat at a seaside diner in upstate Massachusetts. The weather was blowing fiercely outside, and the windows were heavily lashed by relentless whips of rain. We sat cozily tucked away inside and filled our bellies with a lightly cognac-laced oyster bisque that nearly made me cry it was so good. Back to Nanny's declarative statement about pies—this is my own take on that northeast oyster bisque, all turned into a satisfying savory baked dish.

SMOKED SALMON RAREBIT

Serves 4

4 smoked salmon fillets - recipe follows

3 T butter

3 T flour

1 t mustard

1½ c beer

1 lb. cheddar cheese, grated

½ t horseradish

½ t nutmeg

Few drops Tabasco

S&P to taste

1 Melt butter in saucepan over medium heat. Lower heat, whisk in flour and mustard, and cook, stirring for 5 minutes until well-blended. Add beer. Cook, stirring, for about 8–10 more minutes until the sauce settles down and thickens.

2 Add remaining ingredients and cook over low heat 8–10 minutes more.

3 Place smoked salmon fillets in baking dish. Sprinkle 1 T water in dish. Tent and bake at 325° for about 15 minutes to warm. Remove salmon to plates. Top with tomato slices and sauce. Enjoy with roast potatoes, soda bread, and steamed Brussels sprouts or any favorite vegetable.

Every Friday, when I owned my first restaurant, Bandoleone, I used to head down to Pike Place Market—the local farmers' and fishermen's market in Seattle—to buy fresh flowers, fruit, and seafood for the weekend. I would often pick up an already smoked side of salmon, take it home, and after a long weekend of serving folks and playing a gig in there somewhere, cook up a wonderful homey version of salmon rarebit for a late Sunday brunch. That's Americana through and through.

Serves 4

SMOKED SALMON (cont'd)

1 lb. brown sugar

6 to 8 bay leaves

Worcestershire sauce

Rock salt

5 lbs. salmon, filleted

If you're making your own smoked salmon, try this recipe. It's good...

1 Crush the bay leaves by hand and place them into a mixing bowl. Add the brown sugar. Add enough Worcestershire sauce to make a paste out of your sugar mixture. Mix well.

2 Rinse the salmon and pat dry. Cut into 4-inch fillets. Line the bottom of a large casserole dish with a thin layer of rock salt. Rub each salmon piece with a liberal amount of the paste and place the pieces in your casserole dish, leaving a little space between each fillet, ⅛ to ¼ inch or so. When you have filled a single layer in your dish, cover the fillets with a thin layer of rock salt. If necessary, add additional layers on top, alternating fish and rock salt, placing the thickest pieces on bottom and the thinnest on top. Cover with plastic wrap and place in the fridge for 7–8 hours.

3 When the fish is done brining, lightly rinse each piece and place on racks to air dry for about two hours. A nice glaze will form on the fish.

4 Use three to four pans of alder chips in your smoker, smoking the fish for about 8–10 hours.

CHEESE BAKED FISH

Serves 4

2 lbs. fish fillets

¼ c lemon juice

1 T dill

2 T butter

2 c onions, chopped

2 eggs

1 c sour cream

¼ c parmesan, grated

⅓ c Swiss cheese, grated

Nutmeg

S&P

1 Place fillets in lightly oiled baking dish. Sprinkle with lemon, dill, and S&P.

2 In a medium-sized saucepan, sauté onions until soft over medium heat.

3 In a bowl, mix eggs with sour cream, cheeses, S&P, and nutmeg.

4 Top fillets with onions and spoon cream sauce to cover. Bake, uncovered, at 350˚ for about 30 minutes, until the cheese bubbles and fish is cooked through.

My mom bought one of those fondue pots back in the 70s. Then she got creative, trying to make different recipes that no one had ever heard of being served in a fondue pot. This recipe reminds me of one of my mom's endeavors, although to tell you the truth, I think baking the fish makes it taste a lot better than fondueing it!

CITRUS BBQ TROUT

Serves 4

4–8 oz. dressed trout

1 t orange zest

1 t grapefruit zest

¼ c orange juice

3 T grapefruit juice

1–2 T fresh tarragon

1 t olive oil

1 medium orange, sliced

Fresh tarragon sprigs

¼ t ea. salt and pepper

1 Combine orange zest, grapefruit zest, orange juice, grapefruit juice, tarragon, and S&P in a small mixing bowl. Place trout in a shallow baking dish. Pour marinade over fish, opening and turning it to make sure the marinade covers every surface. Cover and refrigerate for 1 hour. Drain and reserve marinade.

2 Place trout in an oil-brushed grill basket or piece of aluminum foil. Arrange citrus slices and tarragon sprigs inside the fish. Grill over medium-high heat for 5–6 minutes. Turn fish over. Brush with reserved marinade and grill for another 5–6 minutes until trout flakes easily with a fork. Serve with marinade poured over the top alongside roasted potatoes and fresh slices of watermelon.

★ ★

Many years ago, I lived in my van in Petersburg, Alaska, while I worked at the local cannery. In between fish runs, toward the beginning or end of the season, local fishermen would take pity on us and drop off huge brailers full of locally caught trout. We would gather at tent city and have these enormous feasts, waiting for the next salmon run, and come up with a thousand ways to prepare the fish we had on hand. I want to thank those fishermen for feeding us and for giving me the impetus to get creative in the kitchen.

SOUR ORANGE TUNA

Serves 4

4 tuna steaks (1½ lb.) cut ½-inch thick

¼ c soy sauce

3 cl garlic, minced

¼ c orange juice

1 t ground ginger

2 T lime juice

4 strips preserved lemon

3 T honey

2 T sesame oil

1–2 T sesame seeds

1 Whisk together all the ingredients except for the sesame seeds and tuna in a mixing bowl. Place the tuna in with the marinade and turn to coat thoroughly. Cover and refrigerate for at least one hour, turning the steaks once or twice.

2 Grill the steaks on a lightly oiled grill over very high heat for about 1 minute per side, or until cooked to your taste. Sprinkle tuna with sesame seeds and serve with rice and vegetables. Pour the remaining marinade over everything and enjoy.

I'd originally intended this marinade for a few pieces of chicken we needed to cook up. But as I ran to the store to pick up a few things, I saw this gorgeous piece of fish on sale and changed my mind. I marinated the fish for nearly two full days since we had to eat that chicken anyway, impressing the flavors deeply into its firm flesh. Jorge insisted I write the recipe down—he was that impressed. The next time I made this, we only marinated the fish for about an hour, and it was just as good.

Serves 4

MARGARITA SALMON

4 salmon fillets or steaks

6 T butter

1 c mushrooms, sliced

2 shallots, chopped

2 cl garlic, minced

2 T cilantro, chopped

2 oz. lime juice

1–2 t flour

$^2/_3$ c tequila

4 T cream

1 nectarine or peach, sliced

4 T parmesan cheese, grated

4 T triple sec

3 T sour cream

S&P

Tabasco

1 In a large, heavy skillet, sauté mushrooms, shallots, and garlic in butter until soft and onions just turn translucent over medium heat. Add S&P and Tabasco to taste, along with cilantro and lime juice. Stir to blend flavors well.

2 Lightly flour salmon and add to skillet. Cook fish until lightly seared.

Add tequila to pan. As the sauce thickens slightly, add cream and fruit. Stir to mix evenly for a minute. Add parmesan and triple sec. Allow to cook, stirring ingredients slightly, but not disturbing the fish too much, for another few minutes.

3 Remove from heat, stir in sour cream to blend, and serve.

★ ★

I used to own a couple of Latin-inspired restaurants in Seattle, Washington. One of our claims to fame, among others, was our immense selection of tequilas—about 100. One afternoon, I was sitting at the bar going over the tequila menu when a fish delivery came in. I put two and two together and came up with this dish.

TUNA NOODLE CASSEROLE

Serves 4

1 can tuna

1 can cream of mushroom soup

14 oz. peas

½ c sour cream

3 c wide noodles

S&P to taste

1 Boil a large saucepan of water. Add a pinch of salt and cook noodles over high heat until just soft. Drain.

2 Flake tuna in a mixing bowl. Add soup, peas, and sour cream. Add cooked noodles, S&P, and stir to combine. Spread mixture into a baking dish and bake at 350˚ for about 30 minutes, until the top of the casserole turns brown and lightly crusty in places. Allow to cool for a few minutes before serving to allow the casserole to settle down.

Who doesn't have a recipe tin with at least one casserole in it? Whether you already have this time-honored Americana dish in your file or not, here's my grandma's version, a dish that got them through hard times during WWII. The casserole doesn't remind me of hard times, though. It simply reminds me of home cooking, through and through.

Crab Cakes

CRAB CAKES

Serves 4

1 lb. crabmeat

2 strips bacon, chopped

2 shallots, minced

½ red bell pepper, chopped

½ green bell pepper, chopped

1 cl garlic, minced

1 celery rib, chopped

¼ c mixed fresh herbs—parsley, cilantro, basil, thyme

4 T fine bread crumbs

Pinch cayenne

1 egg, beaten

2 T heavy cream

3 T butter

S&P to taste

1 Fry bacon in a skillet over medium heat until lightly browned, about 2 minutes. Add shallots, bell peppers, garlic, and celery and cook until soft, about 2 minutes more. Transfer to mixing bowl and let cool.

2 Stir in cleaned crab, herbs, bread crumbs, S&P, and cayenne. Fold in egg and cream. Moisten your hands and form mixture into 4 large or 8 small patties. Wrap in wax paper and refrigerate for about 30 minutes.

3 Heat butter in skillet and pan-fry crab cakes until crusty and golden brown, about 3 minutes per side. Serve with the following sauce:

4 t prepared mustard
1 t A-1 sauce
1 c mayonnaise
2 T half and half
2 t Worcestershire sauce
Salt & cayenne pepper to taste

4 Whisk all ingredients together. Refrigerate until ready to serve.

★ ★

There are a myriad of ways to prepare good crab cakes, from Baltimore to Miami, and Juneau to San Diego, as Americana as it gets. Here's my slightly spiced-up version, keeping in line with where we live today, Texas-style!

Desserts

What's a fine home-cooked meal without something sweet to bust your gut when done? From my favorite cookies to puddings, cupcakes and cakes, pies and ice cream, there's a little something here for every form of sweet tooth. And, however you slice it, it's all Americana to me.

BLACKBERRY CORN CUPCAKES WITH PEACH FROSTING

Makes 12–14

½ c soft butter

16 oz. sour cream

1 c sugar

2 c cornmeal

1 T lemon juice

1 t vanilla extract

5 eggs

2 c blackberries

FROSTING:

1 peach, chopped

¾ c soft butter

32 oz. powdered sugar

1 Cream butter, sour cream, and sugar. Beat until fluffy. Add cornmeal and stir to blend.

2 Add lemon juice and vanilla extract. Stir well. Add eggs, 1 at a time. Fold in blackberries.

3 Spoon batter into tins lined with paper baking cups, ¾ full. Bake at 450˚ for 15–17 minutes, until cupcakes are nicely golden brown.

4 Meanwhile, process peach in processor until pureed. Beat butter in mixer until creamy. Add ¼ of the sugar and beat, then ¼ pureed peach and beat, alternating and beating until creamy and well-blended.

5 When the cupcakes have cooled enough not to melt the frosting, frost each one generously and enjoy.

I like to make these up first thing in the morning and have one freshly frosted alongside a hot cup of coffee while I write. Something about the blackberries, peaches, and corn inspires me—what can I say? Otherwise, yup, they're considered dessert, and most folks eat them up that way, especially after a rowdy backyard BBQ among friends.

CRUMBLE COFFEE CAKE

Serves 6–8

1½ c graham crackers, crushed

¾ c walnuts, crushed

¾ c brown sugar

1 t cardamom

1 c butter, ½ melted, and ½ softened

2 c flour

1 c sugar

2½ t baking powder

½ t salt

2 eggs

1½ t vanilla

1 c milk

2 c fruit—berries, peaches, etc.

1 Preheat oven to 350˚. Butter and lightly flour a 12-inch Dutch oven.

2 Combine first 4 ingredients with melted butter.

3 Combine flour, sugar, baking powder, and salt. Mix well. Add softened butter, eggs, vanilla, and milk and stir until well-blended.

4 Spread half the wet batter into a Dutch oven. Sprinkle half the streusel mixture over the top. Distribute fruit—cherries, berries, peaches, or whatever you're using—cut into ½-inch pieces, over the top. Spread another layer of the batter over the fruit and another layer of streusel on top of that.

5 Bake for about 1 hour or until toothpick inserted in the center of the cake comes out clean. Allow to cool about 20 minutes before slicing and serving.

6 If cooking over coals, cook with 14 briquets on top and 10 underneath.

There is almost nothing finer than sitting around a campfire with friends and serving up a hearty hunk of freshly baked coffee cake. Makes all the other campers jealous—or makes you mighty popular around the campsite, if you share. I often make this at home to have around for a nice something to go along with our coffee in the morning.

SWEET NOODLE BAKE

Serves 10–12

1 lb. wide egg noodles

6 eggs

1 c sour cream

2 c milk

1 lb. cottage cheese

½ lb. ricotta

½ lb. cream cheese, room temp.

½ c sugar

½ t salt

¼ lb. butter, melted

1 t vanilla extract

1 t cinnamon

1½ c raisins

TOPPING

½ c brown sugar

2 T butter, melted

½ c slivered almonds

1 Preheat oven to 350˚. Grease a 9x13 baking pan. Bring a large saucepan of water to boil. Add a pinch of salt and cook the noodles until just soft, about 5–7 minutes. Drain.

2 Mix eggs, sour cream, milk, cottage cheese, ricotta, cream cheese, sugar, and a ½ t salt until smooth. Add melted butter, vanilla extract, cinnamon, and raisins. Stir to blend well. Add noodles to egg mixture and pour into prepared baking dish.

Bake for about an hour, until lightly browned on top and the egg mixture has set.

3 Halfway through baking, mix topping ingredients in a small bowl and pour over the top of the noodle bake.

4 Remove from oven and allow to cool slightly before cutting into squares and serving.

Grandma used to cook for an army, even though it was often only the two of us and grandpa struggling to get through a meal. And by struggling, I don't mean she couldn't cook. Just the opposite! Our problem was that she would make so much food, and we felt obligated to try to finish as much of it as we could. Nowadays, when I make any of her recipes, I either cut them in half or expect to serve about 8–10 people. Here's Grandma's famous noodle bake, a dessert as tasty cold as it is hot. Feel free to add fruit to the recipe, or eat it up just the way I have it here. An obvious note: this is not diet food!

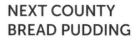

NEXT COUNTY BREAD PUDDING

Serves 4–6

1 Tear bread into medium pieces and place in a large mixing bowl. Add sugar and cinnamon and toss to coat.

2 Mix milk, lightly beaten eggs, and vanilla in a medium-sized mixing bowl. Add to bread mixture. Place ½ mix in casserole. Layer with pecans and raisins. Top with the rest of the mix.

3 Bake at 350° for 30 minutes or until lightly brown.

4 Meanwhile, mix all the sauce ingredients in a small saucepan. Bring to a boil, reduce heat, and cook for another minute, stirring until the sauce thickens slightly. Serve bread pudding warm with bourbon sauce drizzled over the top.

1 lb. French-style bread

¾ c sugar

¼ t cinnamon

3¼ c milk

3 eggs

2 t vanilla

¼ c pecans

¼ c raisins

BOURBON SAUCE:

1 c sugar

6 T butter, melted

½ c buttermilk

2 T bourbon

½ t baking soda

1 T agave syrup

1 t vanilla extract

★ ★

Mom grew up in a dry county. If the family wanted to have a little something to celebrate with, they either had to head over to the next county or know someone who worked a still. This recipe calls for a nice touch of bourbon—hence the name "next county bread pudding." It's devilishly good, and that suits the name too.

CHOCOLATE BOURBON PECAN PIE

Makes 1 9-in. pie

PIE CRUST:

1½ c flour

½ c butter, cold, cut into small pieces

¼ c ice water

½ t salt

FILLING:

1 c sugar

1 c agave syrup

½ c butter

4 eggs, beaten

¼ c bourbon

1 t vanilla extract

¼ t salt

4 oz. choc chips

2 c chopped pecans

½–1 c halved pecans

1 Mix flour and salt in large mixing bowl. Cut in butter with fingertips or two knives, until mixture resembles coarse meal. Add ice water a little at a time and blend with mixture.

2 Turn out onto lightly floured surface and knead until you have a smooth ball. Shape into a slightly flattened disk and roll out to ¼-inch thick. Line pie plate.

3 Preheat oven to 325˚.

4 In a medium-sized saucepan, cook sugar, agave syrup, and butter over low heat until the butter melts and all ingredients are combined. Allow to cool.

5 In a large mixing bowl, combine eggs, bourbon, vanilla, and salt. Add cooled butter mixture and stir to blend.

6 Add chocolate and chopped pecans. Stir to coat. Pour into pie shell. Top with halved pecans in a nice circular pattern. Bake for about 50–55 minutes until the filling has set. Allow to cool before serving.

Every year, a local Austin singer puts together a cancer awareness fundraising event in the form of a Loretta Lynn pie social—one of those events in which gents bid on a pie and then get to eat it while sitting with the gal who baked it. A whole string of other Austin female musicians are invited to participate: We all bake pies and also get up on stage to sing a Loretta song or two. The first year I was invited, I'd been craving chocolate all week and had a mess of pecans sitting on the kitchen counter, so I put the two together and baked what is now my favorite pie of all times. I hope you like it too.

Serves 6

PUMPKIN PIE

PIE CRUST:

2½ c flour

5 T sugar

1 t cinnamon

½ t salt

12 T butter, cold, cut into small pieces

1 T lemon juice

4–5 T ice water

FILLING:

3 eggs

⅓ c sugar

⅓ c brown sugar

2 c pureed pumpkin—canned or fresh

1 t ground ginger

1½ t cinnamon

½ t ea. cloves, allspice, cardamom

Pinch salt

¾ c ea. heavy cream and half and half

1 Process flour, sugar, cinnamon, and salt in a food processor with a steel blade just to combine. Add the butter and process until mixture resembles coarse meal. With the machine running, add lemon juice and water, processing just until a ball forms. Wrap in wax paper and refrigerate a few hours or overnight.

2 Beat eggs and sugar together until light. Stir in pumpkin puree, spices, and salt and mix thoroughly. Stir in cream and half and half.

3 Roll dough out on lightly floured surface to ¼ inch thick. Line 9-inch pie plate. Roll remaining dough out and cut various shapes from dough—leaves, flowers, whatever cookie cutter shapes you have on hand.

4 Pour filling into pie crust. Bake at 450˚ for 8 minutes, then reduce heat to 325˚ and bake another 20 minutes, or until filling is slightly set. Arrange cut-out pie dough in the center or in patterns around the pie and bake another 20–25 minutes until a toothpick inserted in the center comes out clean. Cool completely before serving.

★ ★

The best part of Thanksgiving is when you think you couldn't possibly stuff another bite into your mouth and then someone brings out the pies. Somehow, there's always room for just a little bit more. This is my good old-fashioned basic pumpkin pie, with a cinnamon crust to give it a little extra kick.

GINGER SNAPS

Makes 3 dozen

⅔ c vegetable oil

1 c sugar

1 egg

4 T molasses

2 c flour

2 t baking soda

1 T ginger

1½ t cinnamon

½ t dry mustard

½ t salt

1 Preheat oven to 375˚. In a large mixing bowl, combine oil, sugar, and egg. Add the molasses and stir to combine well. Add the dry ingredients: flour, soda, ginger, cinnamon, mustard, and salt. You should now have a moist dough.

2 Pour a small amount of sugar into a small bowl, about half a cup. Mold the cookie dough into small balls—about 1 inch in diameter—and roll them around in the bowl of sugar. Flatten them slightly and arrange 2 inches apart on an ungreased cookie sheet. Bake for 10 minutes.

3 Spatula the cookies off and allow them to cool on a rack.

During the war, Grandma had to alter recipes to do without butter. Those recipes are lost, but after she told me about those days, I experimented on my own and came up with these incredibly delicious ginger snaps, made with vegetable oil. One bite and you can't tell.

GRILLED SHORTCAKE WITH BRANDIED WHIPPED CREAM AND FRUIT

Serves 4

1 Butter 9-inch cake pan. Preheat oven to 375˚. In small bowl, stir 1 T sugar with cinnamon and set aside.

2 In a large mixing bowl, whisk flour, sugar, baking powder, nutmeg, salt, and baking soda together. Cut in butter until a coarse meal forms. Make a well in the center of the meal and add buttermilk and eggs. Stir with a fork until dough forms. Scrape into cake pan. Bake 35 minutes or until golden brown.

3 In small bowl, pour brandy over raisins. Let stand 20 minutes.

4 Melt butter in a medium-sized skillet. Add peaches or cherries and cook over low heat until just soft, about 6 minutes. Reserve 1 T brandy from the raisins. Add the rest of the brandy and raisins, brown sugar, and cinnamon to the skillet. Cook until crispy in bits yet tender in others, about 7 8 minutes.

5 In medium bowl, whip cream with reserved brandy and a few tablespoons of powdered sugar if you like.

6 Slice shortcake and grill slices over medium-high heat until marks form on the cake. Remove cake from the grill and sprinkle with cinnamon sugar.

7 Spoon peaches or cherries over sliced cake, top with whipped cream, and say "ahhhhh..."

½ c sugar + 1 T

¼ t cinnamon

2 c flour

2 t baking powder

½ t nutmeg

½ t salt

¼ t baking soda

1 stick butter, cold, cut into small pieces

¾ c buttermilk

2 eggs

FILLING:

3 T brandy

¼ c raisins

3 T butter

4 peaches, sliced, or ½ lb. cherries

½ c brown sugar

¼ t cinnamon

1 c heavy whipping cream

★ ★

A friend once told me he could grill anything. When I challenged him to a test, he prepared dinner for his wife and me entirely using the grill: grilled salad, grilled chicken, grilled vegetables, and grilled cake. I immediately returned home and dreamt up this version of that dessert.

BURNT SUGAR ICE CREAM

Makes 1 ½–2 quarts

10 egg yolks, room temperature

¼ t salt

1 c sugar

¾ c water

3½ c milk

1 c heavy whipping cream

1 Beat yolks and salt in a bowl until pale yellow and creamy.

2 In a medium-sized saucepan, boil sugar with ¼ c water over medium heat until golden brown caramel color starts to form. Remove from heat.

3 In another pan, boil ½ c water and add to syrup. Put back on moderately high heat. Scrape sides of pan to keep sugar from gathering there. Boil about 2–3 minutes and remove from heat.

4 Whisk hot syrup into yolks a little at a time until creamy. Let cool.

5 In a large pot, scald milk and cream. Turn off heat. Add 1–2 T to egg mixture. Blend well. Then pour back into milk mixture and cook over low heat, stirring constantly until custard coats the back of a wooden spoon.

6 Let cool. Freeze the mixture in an ice cream maker to manufacturer's directions.

One of my pastry chefs a long time ago used to make burnt sugar concoctions, caramelizing everything she could set her hands on. I love making homemade ice cream and was inspired to create this oh-so-tasty special treat.

PEANUT BUTTER CHOCOLATE CHIP ICE CREAM

Makes 1 quart

1½ c milk

1½ c heavy whipping cream

½ c brown sugar

6 egg yolks

1 c unsalted peanuts, pureed until fine

⅓ c peanut butter

½ c chocolate chips

1 Heat the milk and cream in a medium-sized saucepan until hot but not boiling.

2 Beat the sugar and egg yolks in a large mixing bowl until a slowly dissolving ribbon forms when the beaters are lifted. Slowly pour the hot milk and cream into the sugar mixture, beating constantly. Pour the entire contents of the bowl into the saucepan and return to heat on low, stirring constantly, until thick enough to coat the back of a wooden spoon. Remove from heat and cool.

3 Stir the pureed peanuts and peanut butter into the mixture. Process until smooth. Add chocolate chips and stir to evenly distribute.

4 Freeze the mixture in an ice cream maker to manufacturer's directions.

★ ★ ★ ★ ★ ★ ★ ★ ★ ★ ★ ★ ★ ★ ★ ★ ★ ★ ★ ★

Jorge's favorite flavors in the whole world are a well-made peanut butter cookie with chocolate chips. Here's a great summer version of those favorite Americana flavors for everyone to enjoy.

NANNY'S CHOCOLATE PUDDING

Serves 6–8

2 c milk, heavy whipping cream, or half and half

8 oz. chocolate

½ c sugar

6 egg yolks, room temperature

1 t vanilla extract

Pinch salt

1 In a double boiler or heavy saucepan, heat milk, and chocolate until smooth and well-blended.

2 Whip egg yolks and sugar in processor then pour hot chocolate into eggs, a little at first, then all of it. Blend until smooth and thickened some. Add vanilla and stir to blend.

3 Pour into dessert cups halfway up the side of the cup. Chill an hour or overnight. Serve with whipped cream.

The very best Christmas ever was the year that Nanny made homemade pudding. Not the kind you get in a box and mix up, but real honest-to-goodness, made-from-scratch pudding. There's nothing that says "I love you" like a homemade pudding in my estimation. Try this out on those you love and see what happens.

Makes 1 10-in. pie

CHOCOLATE CHEESE TART

CRUST:

½ c butter

½ c sugar

1 egg

¼ c sour cream

½ t vanilla

2 c flour

½ t baking soda

½ t salt

FILLING:

1½ c ricotta cheese

½ c sugar

2 eggs

½ t vanilla extract

2 oz. semi-sweet chocolate, grated

1 Cream butter and sugar together in a large mixing bowl. Mix in egg, sour cream, and vanilla. Sift flour, soda, and salt into bowl and mix well to form a soft dough. Place in fridge 1 hour.

2 Preheat oven to 350˚.

3 Beat ricotta until smooth. Add sugar, eggs, vanilla, and grated chocolate. Blend well.

4 Flour hands and pat chilled dough into the bottom and sides of a 10-inch pie plate. It will puff slightly during baking, so don't panic when that happens!

5 Pour in filling and bake about 40 minutes, until the filling is set and bounces back lightly when tapped with a finger. Let cool a good 2 hours before serving.

★ ★

I went through a chocolate phase a few years ago, when everything got a hint of chocolate thrown into it. You name it—steaks, eggs, wine, salad, everything got the chocolate treatment. This is my take on a standard cheesecake, changed up a bit to include chocolate in a very tasty way. Sit back and enjoy some toe-tapping music when you bite into your first slice of this pie.

Thanksgiving Dinner

This is my favorite meal of all time to cook and, better yet, enjoy the leftovers for days afterward. Here are the recipes I've honed and create every year at our house. Hope you love the combination of savory and sweet flavors as much as our family and friends do.

ROAST TURKEY WITH MAPLE HERB BUTTER AND CIDER GRAVY

Serves 12

14-lb. turkey

2 c apple cider

⅓ c maple syrup

2 T fresh thyme or 2 t dried

2 T fresh marjoram or 2 t dried

1½ t grated lemon peel

¾ c butter, room temp.

2 c onion, chopped

1 c chopped carrot

1½ c chopped celery with leaves

2 c mushroom broth—chicken will do

1 t flour

Bay leaf

1 c apple brandy or apple jack

1 Boil cider and maple syrup in heavy saucepan over medium-high heat until reduced by ½, about 20 minutes.

2 Mix in thyme, ½ marjoram, and lemon peel. Add butter and whisk until melted. Season with S&P. Refrigerate about 2 hours, covered.

3 Place rack in lower third of oven and set at 375˚. Pat bird dry. Loosen skin around breast by inserting your hand under the skin. Rub ½ cup maple syrup mix under breast and ½ cup outside all over bird.

4 Stuff bird. Reserve remaining maple syrup mix for gravy.

5 Arrange onions, carrots, celery, and giblets around turkey in roasting pan. Sprinkle with remaining thyme and marjoram.

6 Pour 2 c broth into pan. Roast turkey 30 minutes. Reduce heat to 350˚, cover bird loosely, and roast until thermometer inserted into thick part of breast meat reads 180˚—about 3 hours. Baste occasionally.

7 Remove turkey, tent, and let stand.

8 To make the gravy, strain pan juices into a medium-heavy saucepan. Add broth to equal 3 cups. Bring to boil over medium-high heat.

9 Add 3 T maple butter mix and flour together in a cup. Whisk to form paste. Add to broth mix. Add fresh thyme and bay leaf. Boil until reduced to sauce consistency, whisking occasionally, about 10 minutes. Add apple brandy and cook 5 minutes more, stirring. S&P to taste.

There's nothing that says "Americana home" more than the scent of a roast turkey in the air. Well, that and the sound of a football game on in the background. But at our house folks show up with guitars in hand, and generally before and after dinner we all serenade one another by passing the guitar around and singing songs to and with each other. That's a lot to be grateful for, right there. Any leftovers you might have of this turkey remind you that much more.

WILD MUSHROOM STUFFING

1 Combine hot water and porcini mushrooms in small bowl. Let stand until mushrooms are soft, about 30 minutes. Drain, reserving the liquid, and chop coarsely.

2 Preheat oven to 325˚. Bake bread cubes on sheets until golden brown, turning once, about 15 minutes. Cool and transfer to large mixing bowl.

3 Melt butter in heavy Dutch oven on medium-high heat. Add leeks, shallots, and other mushrooms and sauté about 15 minutes until golden brown. Add celery and porcini mushrooms and sauté additional 5 minutes. Add to bread mix in bowl.

4 Add parsley, hazelnuts, spices, S&P, apples, and cranberries. Toss evenly. Add eggs just prior to stuffing the bird. Mix to coat stuffing evenly with egg.

5 Stuff bird and place remaining stuffing in a buttered baking dish. Add ½ c porcini broth. Cover with foil and bake about 30 minutes. Uncover and bake additional 15 minutes, until slightly crunchy on top and browned.

Every year at Thanksgiving, I round up as many of our friends as possible and put on a huge feast. This is not only my favorite holiday to cook for, but also my favorite leftovers to enjoy for days afterward. I created this stuffing with the incredible bounty of wild mushrooms we enjoyed in the northwest during my years living, cooking, and making music there. The stuffing alone makes me wish Thanksgiving came two or three times a year.

2 c hot water

1 oz. dried porcini mushrooms

1½ lbs. egg or cornbread, cut into ¾-inch cubes

6 T butter

4 c leeks, chopped

1 c shallots, chopped

1¼ lbs. crimini mushrooms, sliced

½ lb. shiitake mushrooms, sliced

2 c celery, chopped

1 c parsley, chopped

1 c hazelnuts, chopped

3 T dried thyme

2 T dried sage

½ lb. apples, chopped

1 c dried cranberries

2 eggs

GLAZED PEARL ONIONS WITH ALMONDS AND RAISINS

Makes 8 Servings

2 lbs. pearl onions

1 c dry sherry

½ c raisins

¼ c honey

¼ c water

2 T butter

1 t dried thyme

⅔ c slivered almonds

4 T sherry wine vinegar

1 Boil pot of salted water in medium pot. Add onions and cook 3 minutes. Drain and cool. Cut root ends of onions and squeeze the onion out of its outer skin from the stem end.

2 Combine onions, sherry, raisins, honey, water, butter, and thyme in heavy skillet or saucepan. Bring to boil over medium-high heat. Reduce to low, cover, and simmer until liquid evaporates and onions caramelize, about 45 minutes.

3 Season with S&P and remove from heat. Re-warm before serving and toss in almonds and sherry wine vinegar.

Another one of my grandma's relishes I fondly recall is a version of this dish. Of course, she would serve it up with cow tongue, which I can't figure how I ever liked. I've added a few ingredients to pair perfectly with your roast turkey. This can be made a day ahead to cut back on Thanksgiving labor and keeps for weeks in the fridge, although I doubt there will be that much left over.

Serves 8

GREEN BEANS-N-PECANS

1 Cook beans in salted water until just tender, about 5 minutes. Drain and rinse in cold water.

2 Melt butter in heavy skillet or saucepan on high. Add beans and toss until heated through, about 4 minutes. Add oil and toss. Season with S&P. Add pecans, parsley, and lemon zest. Toss and serve.

2 lbs. green beans

2 T butter

2 T walnut oil

1 c pecans or walnuts

2 T parsley

1 T lemon zest

S&P to taste

★ ★

I like the way the pecans dress up the beans without making this dish too fancy. It's still recognizable and feels like home.

SIMPLE MASHED POTATOES

Serves 8

3 lbs. Yukon Gold potatoes, quartered length-wise

1 t salt

½ c heavy cream

4 T butter

½ c buttermilk

2–4 cl garlic, minced

S&P to taste

1 Put potatoes into a saucepan. Add salt and water until potatoes are covered. Bring to boil, reduce heat, and simmer, covered, 15–20 minutes, or until done—a fork can easily be poked through them.

2 Drain water from potatoes and move to a large mixing bowl. Use potato masher to mash potatoes until well-mashed. Add cream and butter. Use a strong spoon to beat further, adding buttermilk to achieve the consistency you desire. (Do not over-beat or your potatoes will get gluey.) Add garlic, mix again, and S&P to taste.

The beautiful thing about these potatoes is that you can add just about anything to them to dress them up a little. Some years I add chipotles with a spoonful of the sauce they're packed in. Other years, I add horseradish. And still others, I leave the recipe alone and allow the potatoes to speak for themselves! I also like to leave the skins on to give the mash a bit of interesting consistency. If you prefer your potatoes without skins, go ahead and skin them before boiling.

Serves 4–6

MAC-N-CHEESE

1 Preheat the oven to 350°. In a large pot bring the water to a rolling boil. Add the salt. Add macaroni and stir occasionally. Cook until the macaroni is still firm, 8 to 10 minutes. Drain the noodles and set aside.

2 In the same pot bring the cream, garlic, and broth to a simmer. Add the mustard, 3 c gruyere, and nutmeg. Season with S&P to taste. Simmer gently, stirring constantly, until the cheese is melted and mixed well with the cream. Add the parmesan and cheddar. Stir and simmer again until smooth. Add a splash of Worcestershire and a splash of hot sauce. Stir to blend.

3 Add the macaroni to the cream and mix gently. Allow the macaroni to rest on the stove, 5 to 10 minutes.

4 Fill a baking dish with the macaroni mixture, top with bread crumbs, the remaining gruyere cheese, and bake 10 to 12 minutes or until the bread crumbs crust on top. Serve immediately.

10 c water

3 c elbow macaroni

1 qt. heavy cream

2 cl garlic, crushed

1 c broth—mushroom or vegetable work well

2 T Dijon mustard

3½ c grated gruyere

½ t nutmeg, grated

½ c finely grated parmesan

½ c grated sharp cheddar

Worcestershire sauce, to taste

⅓ to ½ c bread crumbs

S&P

Hot sauce, to taste

★ ★

A few years ago, a friend I'd invited to Thanksgiving dinner informed me that she was a vegetarian. Since she still ate dairy, I made up this Thanksgiving mac-n-cheese just for her. But by the time the platter reached her plate, there was hardly any left! Now I make this every year, as folks just seem to expect it.

CITRUS CRANBERRY SAUCE

2 c cranberries

1 c dried cranberries

1 c dried cherries

Juice and chopped zest of 1 orange

1 T dry mustard

¼ c port

½ c sugar, or more if needed

1 t cinnamon

1 T cornstarch

1 In a small saucepan combine cranberries, cherries, orange juice and zest, mustard, port, sugar, and cinnamon. Bring to a boil, reduce heat to simmer, and cook until cranberries are tender, stirring occasionally.

2 In a small cup mix cornstarch and 1 tablespoon water. Whisk cornstarch mixture into cranberry sauce and cook, whisking, until sauce thickens. Taste and add more sugar, if necessary.

Every year, my mom would lay out this enormous feast, and all our "orphan" friends would come over for a rollicking dinner. Afterward, we would sit on the back porch and sing songs late into the night, accompanied by our friends on guitar, fiddle, and banjo. By the time we'd finished singing, everyone would be hungry again, so we would make up sandwiches of turkey and onions with this cranberry sauce for the road. Sometimes the road merely led them to a couch or the hammock out back, but either way, in my memory, this sauce always ended the night.

Outro

Now that you've enjoyed some of the fine taste sensations and completely enjoyable sounds at Ruby's Juke Joint, we hope you move on down the road with a bigger smile on your face than when you arrived.

Just make sure you stop on by every so often to say howdy to the folks around here. We'll keep you in mind wherever we go and while enjoying whatever new dishes and songs we dream up next.

Until next time, keep on cookin'!

Ruby Dee

Index

7-Up 17

A

Agave syrup 141, 142
Ale 43
Allspice 84, 93, 103, 143
Almond(s) 35, 37, 38, 52, 53, 83, 140, 154
Apple(s) 53, 57, 83, 102, 121, 122, 153
- brandy 152
- cider 152
- cider vinegar 56
- fritters 91
- Jack 152
- roasted quail 114
Applesauce 92, 114
Apricot(s) 92, 109
Artichoke(s) 47, 83, 120
Asparagus 31
Avocado 53

B

Baby Back Ribs with Apricot BBQ Sauce 109
Bacon 29, 52, 56, 78, 102, 103, 104, 114, 135
- and blue cheese vinaigrette 74
- wrapped dates 38
Baked beans 45, 56
Baking powder 42, 60, 61, 80, 84, 90, 91, 92, 93, 94, 139, 145
Baking soda 30, 31, 56, 61, 62, 90, 92, 94, 141, 144, 145, 149
Balsamic vinegar 38, 47, 63, 69, 106
Banana(s) 44, 98
- cheese pies 36
Bandoleone 128
Basil 45, 95, 123, 124, 135
Bay leaf 33, 56, 66, 104, 109, 112, 129, 152
Beans 103
- black 26, 51
- green 45, 53, 155
- kidney 66
- navy 56
- pinto 66

Beef
- ground 46, 96, 105
- short ribs 111
- sirloin ground 29
- sirloin steak 107
- tenderloin 30, 106
- top loin 106
Beer 43, 45, 66, 103, 128
- glazed ribs 110
Beet(s) 34, 86
- salad 48
Bell pepper 124
- green 37, 135
- red 34, 37, 135
Bison 103
Black bean(s) 51
- dip 26
Black Eyed Pea and Artichoke Salad 47
Black tea 20, 22, 115
Blackberry (ies) 139
- corn cupcakes with peach frosting 138
Blueberry (ies) 33, 98, 139
- glaze 69
- scones 90
Blue Cheese, Pecan, Apple-Stuffed Bacon-Wrapped Pork Chops 102
Bourbon 17, 18, 61, 109, 141, 142
Brandy 21, 122, 127, 145
Bread crumbs 79, 105, 116, 119, 124, 135, 157
Breakfast Pie 97
Broth 42, 43, 44, 45, 46, 56, 81, 102, 104, 107, 114, 117, 152, 153, 157
Brown sugar 56, 57, 62, 63, 66, 67, 68, 72, 103, 110, 112, 115, 121, 129, 139, 140, 143, 145, 147
Brussels sprouts 85
Buffalo 103
Burnt Sugar Ice Cream 146
Butter 29, 35, 36, 38, 43, 44, 45, 59, 60, 61, 62, 69, 70, 84, 85, 90, 93, 94, 97, 102, 104, 106, 107, 112, 116, 117, 120, 124, 127, 128, 130, 133, 135, 138, 139, 140, 141, 142, 143, 145, 149, 152, 153, 154, 155, 156

Buttermilk 44, 61, 62, 90, 94, 95, 96, 124, 141, 145, 156

C

Cabbage, green/red 49, 78
Campfire Cornbread 60
Canola oil 63
Capers 37
Caramelized onions 29
Caraway 47, 49, 50, 78, 110
Cardamom 21, 44, 93, 139, 143
Carrot 26, 31, 34, 42, 45, 49, 53, 85, 104, 114, 124, 127, 152
- spread 28
Catsup 46, 67, 105, 109, 112
Cauliflower 81
Cayenne 28, 43, 44, 118, 119, 122, 123, 135
Celery 26, 42, 45, 46, 116, 135, 152, 153
Celery seeds 50
Cheese
- baked fish 130
- blue 29, 52, 74, 102, 106
- cheddar 35, 36, 43, 46, 81, 83, 96, 97, 116, 124, 128, 157
- cottage 35, 140
- cream 35, 83, 140
- fontina 57
- goat, chevre 29, 53
- gruyere 157
- nut loaf 35
- parmesan 57, 130, 133, 157
- ricotta 35, 140, 149
- smoked cheddar 29
- Swiss 29, 130
Cheeseburger Soup 46
Cherry (ies) 121, 145, 158
- pickled 33
Chicken 37, 70
- apple sausage 53
- fiesta-stuffed 116
- fried 118
- island 121
- lemon baked 120
- peachy 122
- pecan 119

- pot pie 124
- smoked 115
- stew with rosemary
 dumplings 42
- wild mushroom
 stroganoff 123
Chili(es) 82, 109
- BBQ Sauce 67
- chipotle 51, 67, 69
- diced green 60, 97
- jalapeño 66, 97, 103
- powder 26, 65, 72, 83, 97, 103, 116, 119
Chips, tortilla 96
Chocolate 142, 147, 148, 149
- bittersweet 23
- bourbon pecan pie 142
- cheese tart 149
- syrup 106
Cider vinegar 51, 56, 70, 85, 109, 121
Cilantro 51, 116, 133, 135
Cinnamon 21, 28, 33, 44, 58, 72, 83, 91,
93, 103, 108, 140, 141, 143, 144, 145, 158
- apple raisin bread 92
Citrus
- BBQ Trout 131
- cranberry sauce 158
Clove 21, 33, 44, 72, 103, 143
Club soda 21
Coca Cola Baby Back Ribs 112
Coconut, shredded 121
Cognac 127
Coriander 26
Corn 45, 51, 53, 116, 124
- bread 60, 61, 153
- creamed 60
- pudding 84
Cornmeal 60, 61, 81, 93, 94, 127, 138
- waffles 94
Cornstarch 68, 158
Crabcakes 135
Cranberry(ies) 53, 153, 158
Cream 95, 96, 133
Cream cheese 35, 83, 140
Cream of chicken soup 134
Creamy Coleslaw 49
Crumble Coffee Cake 139

Cucumber(s) 48, 50, 53
Cumin 44, 65, 66, 72, 97, 108, 109, 111, 116
Currant(s) 53, 62, 108
- griddle cakes 93
Curry 108

D
Dates 38
Deer 103
Dijon mustard 46, 53, 73, 112, 124, 157
Dill 34, 35, 45, 85, 130
- pickles 32
Drunken Beans 66
Dry mustard 144, 158
Dry vermouth 16
Dumplings 42
Dutch oven 42, 46, 56, 59, 60, 61, 62, 66,
78, 103, 104, 114, 115, 139, 153

E
Egg(s) 32, 34, 42, 57, 60, 61, 62, 65, 80,
84, 90, 91, 92, 94, 95, 96, 97, 105, 118, 119,
127, 130, 135, 138, 139, 140, 141, 142, 143,
144, 145, 146, 147, 148, 149, 153

F
Fennel 117
Fettuccine 123
Fiesta-Stuffed Chicken 116
Flour 30, 31, 32, 36, 37, 42, 46, 60, 61, 65,
78, 80, 84, 90, 91, 92, 93, 97, 107, 117, 118,
122, 124, 127, 128, 133, 139, 142, 143, 144,
145, 149, 152
- unbleached white 62
- rye 94
- whole wheat 62
French-style bread 141
Fried Chicken 118
Fried Dill Pickles 32

G
Garlic 26, 28, 29, 37, 43, 44, 45, 46, 48, 53,
66, 67, 70, 71, 73, 79, 81, 82, 83, 95, 96, 97,
103, 104, 105, 108, 109, 110, 111, 112, 115,
120, 132, 133, 135, 156, 157
- powder 30, 31, 118, 122
Ginger 19, 28, 44, 86, 109, 115, 121, 132,
143, 144

- snaps 144
Glazed Pearl Onions with
 Almonds and Raisins 154
Graham crackers 139
Grapefruit 131
Great Pumpkin Soup, The 43
Green beans 45, 53
- and pecans 155
Green tea 18
Greens- kale, mustard,
 turnip, beet or collard 79
Grilled Corn-Black Bean
 Salad 51
Grilled Shortcake with
 Brandied Whipped
 Cream and Fruit 145
Groundnut Stew 44

H
Half and Half 23, 127, 135, 143, 148
Hazelnuts 153
Hearty Vegetable Bean Soup 45
Heavy whipping cream 135, 143, 145, 146,
147, 148, 156, 157
Home Style Hot Chocolate 23
Honey 44, 103, 115, 132, 154
- lemonade 19
Horseradish 85, 128
- mayonnaise 29, 75
Hot Cha-Cha Onion Rings 65
Hot sauce 32, 118, 157

I
Island Chicken 121
Italian seasonings 95

J
Jalapeño peppers 66, 97, 103

K
Kickstart Hash 95
Kitchen Sink Salad 53
Kiwi 98
L
Lamb
- burgers 108
- pies 37, 71
Layered Sweet Potatoes 59

Leek(s) 45, 85, 104, 127, 153
Lemon(s) 19, 21, 68, 79, 120
- baked chicken 120
- juice 19, 21, 26, 28, 35, 44, 68, 73, 79, 108, 120, 130, 138, 143
- vinaigrette 73
- zest 68, 108, 152
Lettuce
- romaine 53
Lime 67, 70, 109, 132, 133
- ade 16, 17

M
Mac-n-Cheese 157
Madeira 107
Mama's Day Steak 106
Mango 98
Maple
- ginger beets 86
- syrup 59, 86, 103, 114, 152
Margarita Salmon 133
Marjoram 45, 95, 124, 152
Marsala 123
Mayonnaise 49, 75, 135
Meat Loaf 105
Melon 98
Milk 30, 31, 32, 42, 46, 60, 65, 84, 91, 92, 93, 95, 96, 105, 139, 140, 141, 146, 147, 148
Mint 18, 20, 98, 108
- mojo 71
- sun tea 20
- fruit salad 98
Molasses 56, 67, 70, 144
Mushroom(s) 29, 45, 104, 123, 124, 133, 153
Mustard 35, 105, 110, 128, 135
- whole grain 52, 53

N
Nanny's Chocolate
 Pudding 148
Nectarine 133
Next County Bread
 Pudding 141
Noodles
- elbow macaroni 157
- wide 134, 140

Nutmeg 72, 81, 84, 124, 128, 130, 145, 157

O
Okra Relish 82
Old Country Soda Bread 62
Olive(s) 16, 35, 53
- green 37
Olive oil 28, 42, 47, 48, 51, 52, 53, 57, 58, 67, 70, 71, 73, 74, 79, 81, 82, 95, 107, 121, 123, 124, 131
Onion(s) 26, 29, 31, 35, 37, 42, 43, 44, 45, 46, 56, 57, 59, 65, 66, 67, 79, 80, 81, 82, 83, 95, 96, 97, 103, 104, 105, 109, 110, 112, 114, 116, 124, 130, 152
- Green 63
- jam 63
- pearl 154
- powder 118, 122
- red 63
- Vidalia 47
- White 112
- yellow 63, 123
Orange(s) 21, 26, 98, 119, 131, 158
- juice 21, 26, 67, 131, 132, 158
Oregano 34, 51, 95, 97
Oyster Bisque Tart 127

P
Papa's Day Steak 107
Papaya 98
Paprika 57, 58, 65, 72, 83, 104, 111, 116, 124
Parsley 104, 108, 120, 123, 127, 135, 153, 155
Peach(es) 133, 138, 139, 145
- mint nectar 18
- pickled 33
Peachy Chicken 122
Peanut(s) 44, 147
- butter 44, 147
- chocolate chip ice cream 147
Pear(s) 53
Pea(s) 42, 45, 53, 104, 124, 134
Pecan(s) 83, 102, 141, 142, 155
- chicken 119
- cornbread 61
Pickled Cherries 33
Pickled Eggs 34

Pickled Peaches 33
Pineapple
- juice 21, 70
- rum BBQ short ribs 111
- rum sauce 70
Pine nuts 108
Plum(s) 52
Pomegranate Glazed Turkey 117
Pork
- baby back ribs 109, 112
- chops 70, 102
- ground 96
- pork loin 110
Port 69, 158
Potato(es) 45, 46, 53, 95, 104
- apple bake 57
- pancakes 80
- Russet 57
- White Rose 120
- Yellow Finn 124
- Yukon Golds 85, 156
Powdered sugar 138
Preserved lemon 132
Prune(s) 92, 107
Pumpkin
- pie 143
- soup 43

Q
Quail 114

R
Raisin(s) 53, 83, 92, 140, 141, 145, 154
- sauce 68
Raspberry(ies) 98
Red pepper flakes 79
Red wine 21, 37, 104
Red wine vinegar 48, 71

Roast Turkey with Maple
Herb Butter and Cider
Gravy 152
Rosemary 12, 81, 95
Rum, dark 70

S
Sage 105, 153

Salmon 129, 133
Sausage 53, 69, 95, 96, 97
Sautéed Greens 79
Scallions 48
Seltzer water 17
Sesame oil 132
Sesame seeds 115, 132
Shallot(s) 52, 53, 74, 107, 127, 133, 135, 153
Sherry 26, 37, 115, 123, 154
Sherry wine vinegar 52, 53, 74, 79, 154
Simple Mashed Potatoes 156
Sirloin 29, 107
Sliders 29
Smoked Chicken 115
Smoked Salmon Rarebit 128
Snakebite 17
Snakehandlers Migas 96
Snap pea(s) 31
Sour cream 45, 75, 83, 97, 123, 124, 130, 133, 134, 138, 140, 149
Sour Orange Tuna 132
Soy sauce 109, 115, 123, 132
Spiced Sangria 21
Spinach 83
Spinach Salad with Warm Bacon Vinaigrette 52
Sprite 17
Squash 31, 43
- Butternut 81
Steak Fingers 30, 71
Steak Rub 72
Stout 110
Strawberry(ies) 98
String bean(s) 31
Stuffed Tomatoes 83
Sugar 18, 19, 21, 22, 33, 34, 49, 50, 51, 53, 60, 61, 64, 65, 71, 73, 78, 84, 90, 91, 92, 94, 98, 120, 138, 139, 140, 141, 142, 143, 144, 145, 146, 148, 149, 158
Sugared Cucumbers 50
Sweet and Sour Cabbage 78
Sweet Noodle Bake 140
Sweet potato(es) 31, 59
- fries 58
Sweet Tea 22
Sweet wine 69

T
Tabasco 103, 104, 128, 133
Tarragon 45, 123, 127, 131
Tea 18, 20, 22, 115
Tequila 16, 61, 133
Texas Martini 16
Thyme 45, 52, 57, 59, 74, 95, 104, 105, 107, 114, 117, 123, 127, 135, 152, 153, 154
Tomatillo 96
Tomato(es) 37, 45, 46, 53, 66, 82, 83, 96, 97, 103, 109
- jam 29, 64
- paste 37, 46, 104, 107, 109
- sauce 70
- stuffed 83
Tortillas 95, 96
Tortilla chips 96
Triple sec 16, 133
Trout 131
Tuna
- canned 134
- fresh 132
- noodle casserole 134
Turkey 117, 152
Turmeric 44

V
Vanilla extract 61, 138, 139, 140, 141, 142, 148, 149
Vegetable Fingers 31
Vegetable oil 37, 80, 144
Venison 30
- stew 104
Vermouth 16

W
Walnut(s) 35, 83, 139, 155
Walnut oil 155
Wasabi peas 53
White vinegar 33, 34, 49, 50, 67, 68, 78, 79, 83
White wine 45, 102, 118, 122
Wild Game Sweet Chili 103
Wild Mushroom Chicken Stroganoff 123
Wild Mushroom Stuffing 153
Winter Vegetables with Cornmeal Grits 81
Winter Vegetables with Horseradish 85
Worcestershire sauce 30, 31, 32, 43, 47, 67, 70, 103, 105, 109, 112, 118, 129, 135, 157

Y
Yogurt 48, 124

Ruby's Juke Joint Americana Cookbook
Companion CD

We've taken the time to compile songs by some of the best Americana artists out there today to provide you with an awesome sonic backdrop to your own home cookin'. We hope you find these tunes inspiring!

Ruby Dee and the Snakehandlers
Austin, TX

TRACK LISTING

"Deep Fat Fry"
(Jim Stringer)
Performed by Jim Stringer
Little Book Music, BMI

"Hit The Road Ruby (Cookbook Version)"
(Mirko Glaser)
Performed by The Lazy Boys

"Does It Matter"
(Estrada)
Performed by The Modern Don Juans
From the album The Modern Don Juans
Courtesy of Spinout Records
Modern Don Juans Music Publishing, BMI

"Bleecker Street"
(Alan Subola)
Performed by The Vibro Champs
From the album Mr. International
Courtesy of Eclectone Records
Midwest Frozen Publishing, ASCAP

"Freight Train"
(McQueen/Passalacqua)
Performed by Elizabeth McQueen
God Save The McQueen Music, BMI/Reckless Pedestrian Music

"The Great Indoors"
(Monica Passin)
Performed by Lil' Mo and The Monicats
Passin Fancy Music, ASCAP

"Surfin' Hula Honky-Tonk"
(Rick Broussard)
Performed by Two Hoots and a Holler
Rick Broussard, BMI

"Down at Albert Brown's"
(DiDia/Espiritu)
Performed by Rick DiDia and Aireene Espiritu
From the album Ten Ton Feather

"Someone Who Loves You"
(Gina Lee)
Gina Lee and the Brisket Boys
Published by GLee Club Music

"Eat My Words"
(Marti Brom)
Performed by Marti Brom and Her Barnshakers
From the album Snake Ranch (Goofin' Records)
Squarebird Music, BMI

"You Can Never Tell (C'est La Vie)"
(Chuck Berry)
Performed by Earle Poole Ball
From the album Live On The Radio
Arc Music, BMI

"I Dreamt"
(L. Tripp)
Performed by Rockin' Lloyd Tripp and the Zipguns
From the album That Crazy New Sound! (Uranium Rock Records)
Lexden Music, BMI

"Home Cookin'"
(Ruby Dee)
Performed by Ruby Dee And The Snakehandlers
Previously unreleased
North Of Bakersfield Music, ASCAP
Produced by Jorge Harada
Engineered by Brendon Bigelow at Raging Steel Fury Studios, Austin, TX
Vocals: Ruby Dee Philippa
Acoustic, electric, and baritone guitar: Jorge Harada
Upright bass: Skip Frontz, Jr.
Drums: Scott French
Fiddle: Sean Orr

"Kitchen Radio"
(Teri Joyce)
Performed by Teri Joyce
From the album Kitchen Radio
Girl Friday Music, BMI

CD Compiled by Ruby Dee Philippa and Jorge Harada in Austin, TX
Summer 2011